Rembrandt to Reno

European Masterpieces from The Fine Arts Museums of San Frar

Australian National Gallery

Rembrandt to Renoir

European Masterpieces from The Fine Arts Museums of San Francisco

Australian National Gallery   National Gallery of Victoria

Indemnified by the Australian Government

Text and photography © 1992 by The Fine Arts Museums of San Francisco
Australian edition © Australian National Gallery, Canberra, ACT 2600, 1992

Cataloguing-in-publication data

Rembrandt to Renoir: European masterpieces from The Fine Arts Museums of San Francisco.

ISBN 0 642 13043 4.

1. Fine Arts Museums of San Francisco — Exhibitions. 2. Painting, European — Exhibitions. 3. Painting — California — San Francisco — Exhibitions. I. Australian National Gallery.

759.940749471

American manuscript edited by Fronia W. Simpson

Australian catalogue edited, designed and produced by the Publications Department of the Australian National Gallery

Typeset by Brown & Co. Typesetters, Canberra
Colour separations by Prepress Services WA Pty Ltd, Perth
Printed by Lamb Printers Pty Ltd, Perth

Contributors to the Catalogue

SAN   Steven A. Nash, Chief Curator, Curator of European Art, The Fine Arts Museums of San Francisco

LFO   Lynn Federle Orr, Curator of European Paintings, The Fine Arts Museums of San Francisco

MCS   Marion C. Stewart, Associate Curator of European Paintings, The Fine Arts Museums of San Francisco

Exhibition Dates

Australian National Gallery, Canberra
14 November 1992 – 31 January 1993
National Gallery of Victoria, Melbourne
19 February – 10 May 1993

Australian Exhibition coordinated by Alan R. Dodge

Presented by American Express International
The Australian National Gallery also acknowledges the generous support of QANTAS Airways Limited, Lamb Printers Pty Ltd, Prepress Services WA Pty Ltd and Australian air Express
Indemnified by the Australian Government

(cover)

Jean Antoine Watteau   *The Foursome. [La Partie quarrée.]*   c.1713   (detail)

ontents

Foreword

Elizabeth Churcher
Director
Australian National Gallery

It is with great pleasure that the Australian National Gallery in Canberra and the National Gallery of Victoria in Melbourne host the Australian tour of this fine group of European paintings from The Fine Arts Museums of San Francisco. The paintings on view to the Australian public provide an overview of more than three hundred years of Western art, centring on French painting from the seventeenth to the nineteenth centuries, but also including Italian, Spanish, Dutch, Flemish and English paintings of the same period. Such an array of fine works would be the envy of any major collection and we feel honoured to receive these important paintings from the San Francisco collections.

The title of the exhibition — *Rembrandt to Renoir* — indicates the vast span of time and the varied creative manifestations that three centuries of European art have produced. While the California Palace of the Legion of Honor, the home of San Francisco's European collection, undergoes earthquake stress-proofing, Australia is the happy recipient of these fine works: they have loaned us their best during reconstruction.

In the past the Australian National Gallery has organized exhibitions to expand the experience of the visitor and put into context Australia's own collections of works from all periods and nations. This exhibition of important images by the great painters of Europe follows on the heels of the exhibition *Esso Presents Rubens and the Italian Renaissance*, which also travelled to Melbourne. Such a fortuitous juxtaposition allows the viewer to continue from the end of the period covered by the Rubens exhibition until well into the nineteenth century: this is a golden opportunity for those who enjoyed *Rubens*. The fine collection of European art held in the National Gallery of Victoria in Melbourne will be particularly complemented by the San Francisco pictures.

We thank the Director of The Fine Arts Museums of San Francisco, Mr Harry S. Parker III, for his early enthusiasm for this project and for his assistance in allowing this great collection to come to Australia. We acknowledge also the outstanding work of Dr Steven A. Nash, Associate Director and Chief Curator, who selected the paintings for Australia and who, with his curatorial team, provided the excellent entries for this catalogue. I also thank Alan R. Dodge, Assistant Director (Public Programs), who acted as co-ordinating curator for the exhibition in Australia. As with all major undertakings, we rely on corporate sponsorship. In this instance we have been joined by American Express International in what should prove to be an exciting and rewarding partnership.

Sponsor's Foreword

Alberto Modolo
President and Region Executive
American Express Travel Related Services
Australia, New Zealand and South Pacific

American Express is delighted to be associated with bringing such a fine exhibition as *Rembrandt to Renoir* to the Australian people.

The exhibition represents a great opportunity to increase our knowledge and understanding of one of the richest collections of European Old Master paintings held in the United States. It is not often that a collection of such range and quality travels outside its home. It is ironic that the misfortune of the Palace of the Legion of Honor, which suffered stress damage in the last major earthquake affecting San Francisco, has meant that we in Australia now have the opportunity to view this outstanding collection.

American Express believes very strongly that the arts play an integral role in enhancing the quality of life for individuals, communities and nations. Our cultural commitment has supported over one hundred and twenty projects in the visual and performing arts in Europe as well as in the United States, Asia, Canada and South America. We are delighted to have the opportunity to support the Australian National Gallery in presenting this important collection to the Australian people.

Preface

Harry S. Parker III
Director of Museums
The Fine Arts Museums of San Francisco

We are delighted to be able to share with Australian audiences so many of the finest European old master paintings from The Fine Arts Museums of San Francisco. Normally housed in the noble architectural setting of the California Palace of the Legion of Honor, one of our two museum facilities, these treasures have been displaced for two years, from 1992 to 1994, by the extensive construction work on the Legion of Honor in the form of seismic reinforcement and important renovations. The inconvenience of closing our building is converted into the unique opportunity to work with the Australian National Gallery and the National Gallery of Victoria on this important collection-sharing program. European painting is one of the strengths of The Fine Arts Museums of San Francisco, and the rich selection composing *Rembrandt to Renoir* includes many of the highlights from these holdings.

The idea for a tour across the Pacific of European masterworks was originally developed with Sir Denys Sutton, who had organized several earlier tours from American museums to Japan. Before his untimely death in 1991, our staff worked with Sir Denys on a selection of sixty-six paintings intended for exhibition at four Japanese museums. The extension of this tour to Australia evolved out of discussions with museum colleagues in Canberra and Melbourne late in 1990.

From the American side of the team that organized the exhibition and its catalogue, we are happy to acknowledge the highly professional co-operation of representatives from the Australian National Gallery and the National Gallery of Victoria. Betty Churcher, Director of the Australian National Gallery, and her fine staff have ably managed many of the logistics of the tour, and James Mollison, Director of the National Gallery of Victoria, has been supportive of the program since its inception.

The production of the exhibition and catalogue demanded the focus, talent and co-operation of many staff members. Steven A. Nash, Associate Director and Chief Curator of European Art, contributed the catalogue's introductory essay and many of the individual entries. Other entries were prepared by Lynn Federle Orr, Curator of European Paintings, and Marion C. Stewart, Associate Curator of European Paintings. Vital to the catalogue effort was the research assistance of Elise L. G. Breall, Curatorial Research Assistant; Stephen Platzman, Intern; and Jerry Smith, Librarian. Fronia W. Simpson served with patience and skill as editor; the Publications Department assisted with aspects of the catalogue; and Suzy Peterson, Secretary to the Chief Curator, performed myriad invaluable duties, including manuscript preparation.

The efforts of Lamar Leland, Coordinator, Photographic Services, and Joseph McDonald, Photographer, produced the admirable photography in the catalogue. Our thanks go also to Debra Pughe, Director of Exhibitions; Therese Chen, Director of Registration; and Sonya Knudsen, Associate Registrar, who contributed their consider-able expertise to the organization of travel arrangements. The care and well-being of the works were entrusted to the paintings conservation staff, including Jim Wright, Pauline Mohr, Cynthia Lawrence and Jennifer Sherman. The objects were expertly packed and crated by Michael Sandgren, Packer.

It is a great pleasure for The Fine Arts Museums of San Francisco to share their treasures with the people of Australia, and we hope their experience in turn will be equally pleasurable.

European Art at
The Fine Arts Museums of San Francisco

Steven A. Nash
Associate Director and Chief Curator
The Fine Arts Museums of San Francisco

Many first-time visitors to San Francisco remark on how European the city seems to them. The relatively compact size of the urban area, its beautiful vistas afforded from numerous high hills, the obvious respect for historical architecture, and one's constant awareness of water and green spaces give San Francisco a special character and evoke comparisons with the great urban centres of Europe. It is only appropriate, therefore, that this most European of American cities should proudly bear in its public domain a collection of European art that ranks as one of the most important in the United States.

Numbering more than nine hundred paintings, five hundred sculptures, twelve thousand decorative art objects in all media, and fifty thousand prints, drawings and photographs, the European collection at The Fine Arts Museums of San Francisco presents a survey of artistic accomplishment from medieval times to the early twentieth century, encompassing works by many of Europe's leading masters. Its history stretches back one hundred years and traces a story of patronage and collection development on the part of innumerable staff members, donors and civic leaders whose work has lent the collections their particular character and strengths. The contributions of these individuals are evident, for example, in the fine array of northern European works from the twelfth to the fifteenth century, in the exceptional Rodin collection, and in outstanding concentrations of Dutch painting and eighteenth-century decorative arts. The exhibition that accompanies this catalogue, presenting the largest group of works from The Fine Arts Museums ever to be seen outside the continental United States, provides a rich sampling of these and other holdings.

The Fine Arts Museums of San Francisco comprise two individual museums joined through merger into a single institution: the M.H. de Young Memorial Museum (fig. 1)

Fig. 1   M. H. de Young Memorial Museum, Golden Gate Park, San Francisco

Fig. 2 California Palace of the Legion of Honor, Lincoln Park, San Francisco

and the California Palace of the Legion of Honor (fig. 2). Founded thirty years apart in two separate city parks, these organizations developed independently, with distinctly different personalities, until legally united in 1972. For each, however, European art figured prominently. Reflective of a cultural attitude, widespread in the United States, that accorded a high value to a Eurocentric view of historical artistic development, weighting this cultural perspective even more than indigenous traditions, both the de Young Museum and the Legion of Honor placed a premium on building their European collections.

From its very beginnings, the Legion of Honor featured a strong transatlantic focus. Founded in 1924 by the local art patrons Adolph Spreckels and his Francophilic wife, Alma de Bretteville Spreckels, the Legion of Honor was based in architectural design on the Palais de la Légion d'Honneur in Paris and included in its early collections many European works donated by Mrs Spreckels and her friends. Although the de Young Museum started as a far more eclectic, multi-purpose institution, it too was born of a strong international spirit.

Thanks largely to the initiative and efforts of Mr M. H. de Young, city leaders in San Francisco were able to organize on the heels of the World's Columbian Exposition of 1893 in Chicago their own major multinational celebration of art, industry and culture. When the California Midwinter International Exposition, popularly known as the Midwinter Fair, opened in Golden Gate Park early in 1894, it included within the vast panorama of foreign and national exhibits a Fine Arts Building housing hundreds of paintings, sculptures, watercolours and drawings. At the close of the fair, its Executive Committee donated to the City of San Francisco the Fine Arts Building (with the understanding that it become a permanent museum), along with funds to help build its collections. M. H. de Young worked to retain from different exhibits at the fair as many interesting artefacts and examples of fine and applied art as possible, and also began buying for the museum. The Memorial Museum, which eventually would bear de Young's name, was inaugurated on 23 May 1895.

The original collection of the Memorial Museum numbered more than six thousand works on display and ran the gamut from geological and natural history items to ethnographic and decorative arts of all descriptions. Most of the works from the original Fine Arts Building had been dispersed, however, and the beginnings of the paintings and sculpture collection were modest. Among the sculptures listed in the museum's 1899 handbook were several works by Paolo Troubetzkoy and lesser artists such as Henri Plé and Orazio Andreoni, as well as the eleven-foot-high bronze vase by Gustave Doré entitled *Poème de la vigne* (fig. 3), which still commands much attention today. Paintings included works by Corot, Diaz, and Benjamin Constant, and a panel attributed to Cima, among other, more minor objects.

Fig. 3 Gustave Doré French 1832–1883 *Poème de la vigne.* 1877–78 bronze height 335.0 cm Signed and dated: *Gve Dore*; stamped: *Thiébaut-Frères-Fondeurs 1877–8* Gift of M. H. de Young 53696

Important additions were made to the museum's facilities in 1919 and 1921. By then the paintings and sculpture collections had grown considerably in size, although the European holdings were dominated by nineteenth-century academic artists. Among the French painters represented were Julien Dupré, Louis Béroud, Charles-François Daubigny, Jules Didier and Georges Jeannin. Works from nineteenth-century Spain and Italy were also included, along with a handful of old master paintings and an interesting group of Russian works. Several paintings of consequence, including Konstantin Makovsky's large *The Russian Bride's Attire* and Bouguereau's *The Broken Pitcher* (cat. no. 56), came to the museum from M. H. de Young's personal collection after his death in 1926.

After these eclectic and earnest but nevertheless limited beginnings, major strides were made in the following decades, due largely to the generosity of certain key donors and the determined guidance of particular directors. One of the guiding forces in these intermediate stages of the museum's history was Walter Heil, who served as Director of the de Young Museum and Legion of Honor jointly from 1933 to 1939 and of the de Young Museum singly from 1939 to 1961. Born and educated in Germany, Heil was an aggressive collector and respected connoisseur, whose tastes ran mainly to medieval and old master European art. His leadership raised the museum from provincial to international status.

With funds from two key sources, the M. H. de Young Endowment Fund and donations from the de Young Museum Society, Heil purchased important tapestries and medieval objects as well as works by such artists as Edmé Bouchardon, Giovanni Battista Gaulli (cat. no. 5), Thomas Gainsborough (cat. no. 19), Corneille de Lyon, Jan Steen (cat. no. 15) and the Master of the Lanckoronski Annunciation, among others. A particularly key work in the collection, Peter Paul Rubens's monumental *The Tribute Money* of about 1612, was purchased with donated funds, bringing to San Francisco one of the few early religious paintings by this master in the United States. Heil was able to acquire through purchase other seminal works such as Corot's superb *View of Rome* (cat. no. 54) and El Greco's beautifully preserved *Saint John the Baptist* (cat. no. 1) and was also instrumental in attracting to San Francisco a donation that radically elevated the quality of the collection: a gift of thirty-nine European paintings from the Samuel H. Kress Foundation in 1961. This outstanding group of works spans the period from the early Renaissance to the nineteenth century, giving representation to many fine artists not previously included in the collection, such as Cesare de Sesto, Luca di Tommè, Pontormo, Titian, Pieter de Hooch (cat. no. 17), Salomon van Ruysdael (cat. no. 10), Giovanni Battista Tiepolo, Claude Lorrain and Goya. Other important sources of benefaction during Heil's tenure were the newspaper magnate William Randolph Hearst and the Hearst Foundation, from whom came the gift of numerous medieval and Renaissance objects and such wonderful examples of European decorative art as the famous seventeenth-century ebony cabinet on stand attributed to Jean Macé (fig. 4).

Equal in importance to the gift from the Kress Foundation, in terms of the overall advancement of the collection, was the involvement of Roscoe and Margaret Oakes as patrons and general supporters. Enthusiasts of European painting and decorative arts, the Oakeses became interested in the museum after World War II and came to rely heavily on the advice of Walter Heil in the building of their personal collection, much of which they kept on long-term loan at the de Young Museum. Through gifts and bequests, the museum eventually benefited magnificently from the Oakeses' collection, with the addition of such masterworks as Dieric Bouts's *Virgin and Child*, Georges de La Tour's *Old Man* and *Old Woman* (cat. nos 25, 26), Hals's *Portrait of a Gentleman in White* (cat. no. 8), van Dyck's *Duchesse d'Havré and Child* (cat. no. 9), Rembrandt's *Joris de Caulerij* (cat. no. 12), Gainsborough's *Landscape with Country Carts* (cat. no. 20), David's *La Baronne Meunier* (cat. no. 47), Cellini's *Portrait of Cosimo I de' Medici*, and

Fig. 4 Attr. to Jean Macé French *c*.1602–1672 *Cabinet on Stand*. after 1641 ebony with inlay of various woods 229.8 x 222.2 x 76.2 cm Gift of William Randolph Hearst 47.20.2

numerous other fine paintings and works of decorative art, particularly French furniture. These gifts at last gave the museum the foundation of European old masters that it badly needed. In addition, the Oakeses provided for an endowment for acquisitions that remains The Fine Arts Museums' single largest purchase fund. Through this source have been acquired many more fine works by artists including Preti (cat. no. 3), Stomer (cat. no. 11), Cima, Grimaldi, Roghman and Valenciennes (cat. no. 48), plus silver, ceramics and furniture. A total of eighteen works have been purchased with the Oakes Fund since its establishment.

During the period briefly surveyed here, from the late 1920s to the 1960s, the California Palace of the Legion of Honor also benefited from a number of salutary gifts. The protracted gestation of the Legion of Honor dates to the Panama-Pacific International Exposition in San Francisco in 1915. Alma Spreckels had dreamed earlier of building a new art museum for the citizens of San Francisco. At the Panama-Pacific Exposition, she and her husband, Adolph, were entranced by the replica of the Palais de la Légion d'Honneur constructed as the French government's pavilion to house among other things an exhibition of Rodin sculpture. Together Alma and Adolph Spreckels resolved to create another reconstruction of this building in more permanent materials for their museum. They chose a site in Lincoln Park high on a hill overlooking the Pacific Ocean, but work on the structure was interrupted by World War I, and it was not completed until 1924.

When the Legion of Honor was inaugurated, it contained primarily a mixture of decorative arts donated or lent by Mrs Spreckels and a few other patrons. Realizing the urgent need to build the collection, Alma Spreckels set out with characteristic energy to secure the gift or purchase of suitable works.

Her own main passion in art was for the sculpture of Auguste Rodin. Through the American-born modern dancer Loïe Fuller, Mrs Spreckels met Rodin in France in 1914, three years before his death. The tutelage of Loïe Fuller in art had aroused Mrs Spreckels's interest in Rodin, and she made her first purchases of his work later in 1914, with Fuller as intermediary agent. Thus commenced a collection that would eventually expand to over eighty works in bronze, stone, plaster and terracotta and that would represent one of the greatest concentrations of Rodin's art outside France (fig. 5). Mrs Spreckels lent works from her collection to the Legion of Honor and eventually gave the collection in its entirety. She also donated eighteenth- and early-nineteenth-century French porcelains and silver, as well as a group of classical ceramics.

Fig. 5 Auguste Rodin French 1840–1917 *The Thinker*. 1880 bronze 198.0 x 129.5 x 134.0 cm Gift of Alma de Bretteville Spreckels 1924.18.1

One of Mrs Spreckels's most important 'acquisitions' for her new institution was the interested participation of Archer M. Huntington, son of the railroad magnate Collis P. Huntington, who had lived briefly in San Francisco and himself had given works to the de Young Museum. In the late 1920s and early 1930s, Archer Huntington donated to the Legion of Honor much of his superb collection of eighteenth-century French art. Consisting of several important sculptures, Sèvres ceramics, and fine pieces of furniture

Fig. 6 Martin Carlin French c.1730–1785 *Cabinet*. c.1770–80 ebony with Japanese lacquer veneer and gilt-bronze mounts 83.4 x 115.5 x 49.5 cm Gift of Archer M. Huntington 1931.145

by such masters as Bernard II van Risen Burgh, Joseph Baumhauer and Martin Carlin (fig. 6), this collection provided the foundation of the Legion of Honor's outstanding representation of French decorative art from the rococo period. Furthermore, with funds that Mr Huntington donated, the museum purchased important paintings from the same era, including works by Fragonard, Largillierre (cat. no. 29), Watteau, Perronneau and Greuze.

Indefatigable in her efforts to attract great works to the Legion of Honor, Mrs Spreckels pursued other collections, including that of Calouste Sarkis Gulbenkian, which eventually went to Portugal. She was more successful with Mr and Mrs Henry K. S. Williams. A native of the San Francisco Bay Area, Mildred Anna Williams had gone East to seek her fortune, and there had married the wealthy businessman Henry Williams. The two established residence on the avenue Foch in Paris, where they accumulated a large collection of European paintings and decorative arts. Mrs Spreckels became friendly with the Williamses during her frequent visits to Paris and finally persuaded them to donate the majority of their art to the Legion of Honor. A deed of gift was signed in 1928. Although the Williamses chose to retain possession of their collection until both were deceased, Mrs Williams died accidentally in 1939, and Mr Williams decided at that time to withdraw the collection from Europe before war broke out and to give it to the Legion of Honor. He continued to buy and donate both American and European paintings in his wife's name until his death in 1944. By then, the Mildred Anna Williams Collection consisted of over eighty paintings, including works by Le Nain (cat. no. 27), Moroni, Snyders, Constable, Gainsborough and Hondecoeter, and other key examples that are still mainstays of the collection. Of equal importance was the establishment by the Williamses of an acquisition fund that enabled the purchase of more than eighty additional paintings over the next thirty-five years. Highlights of these purchases include Renoir's *Landscape at Beaulieu* (cat. no. 65), Degas's *Musicians of the Orchestra* (cat. no. 59), Nattier's *Thalia* and *Terpsichore* (cat. nos 31, 32), Manet's *At the Milliner's* (cat. no. 58), Monet's *Water*

Lilies (cat. no. 63), Cézanne's *Forest Interior* (cat. no. 61), Watteau's *La Partie quarrée* (cat. no. 30), Le Sueur's *Sleeping Venus* (cat. no. 28) and Vouet's *Holy Family with the Infant Saint John*. Such works made an inestimable difference in the Legion of Honor's collection and were especially important in developing the nineteenth-century holdings.

During the era of expansion represented by the growth of the Williams collection, much credit for able stewardship must be given to Thomas Carr Howe, Jr, who served first as Assistant Director of the Legion of Honor from 1931 to 1939 and then as Director from 1939 to 1968. In addition to organizing many fine exhibitions, Howe managed the development of the collection, working closely with donors such as Mrs Spreckels and the Williamses and searching out works for purchase and gift. During his tenure, important donations came from Arthur Sachs (ancient and medieval objects), Catherine D. Wentworth (French silver), the Grace Spreckels Hamilton family (French tapestries and decorative arts) and Mr and Mrs Prentice Cobb Hale (Impressionist paintings), among others. In 1943, Albert Campbell Hooper presented a collection numbering more than three hundred and fifty objects, primarily porcelain, silver and other decorative arts. The donation of several European period rooms provided ambience at the Legion of Honor for its growing collections of decorative arts of different kinds.

With a major gift from Dr T. Edward and Tullah Hanley in 1968, the collection advanced on several fronts, including nineteenth- and twentieth-century paintings, drawings and sculpture. Important oils by Géricault (cat. no. 53), Matisse and Manet, among others, came to the Legion of Honor, as well as such outstanding drawings as Blake's *The Complaint of Job*, Gauguin's *L'Arlesienne* and Monet's *The Coast of Normandy*.

For the prints and drawings collection in general, a monumental step had been taken in 1950 with the establishment of the Achenbach Foundation for Graphic Arts, based on the donation by Mr and Mrs Moore Achenbach of their large collection of old master and modern prints, and bolstered by their gift of an endowment fund for acquisitions. This fund has permitted regular purchases of prints and drawings since 1960. Thanks to these acquisitions and the generosity of innumerable other donors, the Achenbach collection has grown to over one hundred and ten thousand works of art on paper. It is the largest and most comprehensive collection of its type in the western United States.

With the merger of the de Young Museum and the Legion of Honor in 1972 into The Fine Arts Museums of San Francisco, a new era of administration and collecting began. Ian McKibbin White, who had served as Director of the Legion of Honor since 1968, became director of the combined operations, to be followed upon his retirement in 1987 by Harry S. Parker III. Exhibition and collection programs were integrated between the two museums, and a single, unified overview was brought to bear on their development. Certain collecting areas formerly limited in scope, such as African, Oceanic, and Pre-Columbian art, began to grow rapidly, and American art experienced an especially dramatic expansion, thanks primarily to the gift in 1978 of the magnificent collection of paintings belonging to Mr and Mrs John D. Rockefeller 3rd.

European art, however, remained a high priority. Gifts from Hélène Irwin Fagan augmented importantly the tapestry collection and the medieval holdings; a bequest from William H. Noble in 1973 enabled such notable purchases as Seurat's *Eiffel Tower* and Gérard's *Comtesse de Morel-Vindé and Her Daughter* (cat. no. 51), plus several sculptures and pieces of furniture; and particularly important support for English furniture and European ceramics came from Mr and Mrs Robert Magowan and Mr and Mrs Henry Bowles respectively. The Whitney Warren Bequest in 1988 brought several fine works of art plus a purchase fund that underwrote the acquisition of John Martin's monumental *Assuaging of the Waters* (cat. no. 24).

In 1989 a collection reorganization concentrated the European holdings of The Fine Arts Museums at the Legion of Honor. With the collections shown together under one roof for the first time, their continuity and strengths could be appreciated in full. When the Legion of Honor is reopened in 1994 after two years of renovation and seismic strengthening, the 1989 installations will be re-created. Consisting of more than one thousand works of art, they feature a chronological integration of paintings, sculpture and decorative art that presents a contextual picture of succeeding historical periods.

Since the present is always a product of the past, the historical forces that have shaped the one-hundred-year history of The Fine Arts Museums are very much alive in its European installations. Out of this history have come both strengths and limitations. The representation of medieval and early Renaissance art from Germany, France and the Lowlands, for example, is remarkably rich. An exceptional group of early tapestries is augmented by stained glass, sculpture and works in various applied arts from the twelfth to the fourteenth century, leading historically to the beginnings of panel painting as exemplified by key works by Dieric Bouts and the Master of the Saint Lucy Legend (fig. 7).

The gift from the Kress Foundation in 1961 has enriched the Museums with a fine group of early Italian Renaissance gold-ground paintings, and although sixteenth-century art is not a particular strength of the collections, an interesting international introduction to this complex period is presented by such works as those by Cellini, Cesare de Sesto, El Greco, Pontormo and Titian, and a group of very rare paintings and objects from the School of Fontainebleau.

Thanks again to the Kress gift as well as to initial donations and later purchases forming the Oakes and Williams collections, the baroque period is more deeply represented, especially in the Dutch and Flemish field. Rembrandt's engaging portrait of Joris de Caulerij is one of the great art treasures on the West Coast of the United States. Together with outstanding works by Rubens, Hals, Steen, Ter Borch, de Hooch and others, it helps constitute within the collection a subsection of notable distinction.

Since the earliest days of both the de Young Museum and the Legion of Honor, the collecting of decorative arts has been a major theme and pursuit, leading to notable holdings of French and English silver, ceramics and furniture, with good examples also from Germany and Italy. The high point of this tradition is found in the arts of eighteenth-century France, where the Museums' holdings include outstanding examples of work in all media.

Fig. 7   Master of the Saint Lucy Legend   Flemish   active last quarter of fifteenth century   *Virgin and Child Enthroned with Angels*   oil and tempera on panel 79.4 x 52.1 cm   Mildred Anna Williams Collection   1953.38

main concentrations. Works by Watteau, Fragonard, Boucher (cat. nos 35–37), Lancret (cat. nos 33, 34) and Nattier, for example, illustrate beautifully the aesthetic variety and excellence of the rococo period, while portraits by Vigée Le Brun (cat. no. 49), Greuze and Goya, and Valenciennes's wonderful *Capriccio of Rome with the Finish of a Marathon*, show the changing theoretical and stylistic dynamics at the end of the century. Also of especial note is the representation of British painting spanning the eighteenth and nineteenth centuries, seen in works by Gainsborough, Reynolds, Lawrence, Constable (cat. no. 23) and others.

With the nineteenth-century collections, major strengths exist beside key gaps. The great neoclassicist J.-L. David is well represented, as is his pupil Gérard, but French romanticism is manifested only in Géricault's oil sketch of Charles V. The mid-century landscape tradition of the Barbizon school and early Impressionism can be followed in works by Corot, Daubigny, Courbet and Boudin, and wonderful Impressionist paintings by Manet, Degas, Monet, Renoir and Pissarro (cat. no. 57) are included, but Post-Impressionism is not a strong point, aside from Seurat's *Eiffel Tower* and Cézanne's *Forest Interior.*

With the sculpture of Rodin and his contemporaries, the nineteenth-century collection reaches one of its heights. Building on the Spreckels' collection of Rodins, an effort has been made to add works by Dalou, Carpeaux, Degas and Renoir, and to move the collection into the twentieth century with the acquisition of key sculptures by Maillol, Archipenko and Nadelman.

Until recently, twentieth-century art had not been a focus of The Fine Arts Museums except in the collection of prints and drawings. Greater efforts are now being made to trace the major artistic developments of our century through both exhibitions and acquisitions. The great accomplishments of all contributors to the European collections of the de Young Museum and the Legion of Honor over the past century will thus be furthered by extending into new territory the continuum of the historical periods so well represented up to now. This challenge, plus that of strengthening the historical coverage, lies ahead for the next one hundred years of collecting.

Installed in the elegant spaces of the Legion of Honor, these collections create a particularly rich impression, especially seen in conjunction with the eighteenth-century French paintings that make up another of the Museums'

A Note to the Reader

Abbreviations

CPLH = California Palace of the Legion of Honor
de Young = M. H. de Young Memorial Museum
TFAMSF = The Fine Arts Museums of San Francisco
French Paintings = Pierre Rosenberg and Marion C. Stewart, *French Paintings, 1500 – 1825, The Fine Arts Museums of San Francisco*, San Francisco, 1987

Literature and exhibition histories are highly selective. The use of 'to' in provenance connotes direct passage from the previously cited owner. Dimensions are given in centimetres, height before width.

Catalogue

Spanish and Italian Paintings

Doménikos Theotokópoulus, called El Greco
Spanish, 1541–1614

Today considered one of the greatest artists of the Spanish school, El Greco the Greek was actually born in Candia, the capital of Crete, a Greek island then under Venetian control. The artist always acknowledged this origin, signing his works with his given name, Doménikos Theotokópoulus, in Greek characters. The *Kres* appearing in some signatures means 'Cretan'. El Greco's early works demonstrate that he worked within the conservative tradition of Byzantine icon painting before exposure to Venetian High Renaissance art broadened his stylistic approach. In Venice by 1568, he is documented in Rome in 1570, and he remained there until 1577. In Rome he gained entrée into the influential circle of Cardinal Alessandro Farnese and in 1572 was accepted as a miniaturist into the Academy of Saint Luke. Most likely seeking royal patronage, in 1577 El Greco moved permanently to Spain, and by 1579 had completed *The Disrobing of Christ* (*El Espolio*) for the sacristy of the cathedral of Toledo. One of the artist's masterpieces, this painting exhibits the full brilliance of his perfect wedding of a highly idiosyncratic style with the emotional intensity of the Counter Reformation. Although religious works predominate in his oeuvre, El Greco was also a masterful portraitist. Failing to secure a permanent appointment at the court of Philip II in Madrid, El Greco worked the rest of his long career in Toledo, where he died in 1614.

1

Saint John the Baptist. c.1600

Painted around 1600 for the convent of the Descalced (Barefoot) Carmelites in Malagón, where it remained until 1929, this is El Greco's most brilliant depiction of Saint John the Baptist. As discussed elsewhere (see cat. no. 3), the figure of the Baptist has been treated with great frequency in Christian art. The asceticism of John the Baptist, who lived in the wilderness of Judea, made him one of the most popular saints among Spanish mystics. In El Greco's *Saint John the Baptist* the emaciated form of the saint recalls the stylized Byzantine tradition in which the artist was initially trained. This mannerist elongation of the body emphasizes the austere nature of Saint John, considered the last of the Old Testament prophets to preach the coming of the Messiah and the first of the New Testament saints to acknowledge the person of Jesus as that Messiah. To suggest the intense religious zeal of the saint, the painter has activated the entire composition. Broken brushstrokes delineate the undulating forms of man, landscape and clouds, creating a flickering pattern of light. The strident hue of the landscape and cloud-streaked sky behind the figure increases the sense of spiritual energy.

Symbolic of Christ's role as the sacrificial lamb by which the redemption of mankind will be realized, a lamb is shown on an altarlike stone at the Baptist's feet. The lamb seems to clutch a reed with a banderole that reads *[ECCE] AGNUS DEI*, relating to the Baptist's words 'Behold the Lamb of God, who takes away the sins of the world!' (John 1: 29).

LFO

oil on canvas
111.0 x 66.5 cm
Signed in Greek minuscule on rock at lower right:
domenikos theotokopolis e'poiei
Museum purchase, funds from various donors
46.7

Provenance:
Convent of the Carmelitas Descalzas, Malagón (Ciudad Real), until 1929; Felix Schlayer, Madrid; Arnold Seligmann Rey & Co., New York, 1940; Rudolf J. Heinemann, New York; purchased by the de Young, 1946.

Literature:
Gianni Manzini and Tiziana Frati, *L'opera completa del Greco*, Milan, 1969, no. 118, repr.; Jose Gudiol, *El Greco*, New York, 1973, no. 151, fig. 178; Edi

Baccheschi and Ellis Waterhouse, *El Greco: The Complete Paintings*, London, 1980, no. 105a, fig. 105a.

Exhibited:
San Francisco, CPLH, *Seven Centuries of Painting*, 1939–40, no. L-24;
New York World's Fair, *Masterpieces of Art*, 1940, no. 111;
San Francisco, de Young, *Loan Exhibition of Masterworks by El Greco*, 1947, no. 12, repr., colour cover;
The Denver Art Museum, *Baroque Art: Era of Elegance*, 1971, p. 102, repr. p. 103;
Madrid, Museo del Prado; Washington, DC, National Gallery of Art; The Toledo Museum of Art; Dallas Museum of Fine Arts, *El Greco of Toledo*, 1982, no. 37, fig. 37, colour pl. 52.

Massimo Stanzione
Italian, c.1585–1658

The eighteenth-century biographer Bernardo de Dominici, our primary source for information regarding the career of Massimo Stanzione, states that the artist was born in Orto di Atella in 1585. He spent most of his active career in Naples, where it is reported he trained with Fabrizio Santafede and Giovanni Battista Caracciolo, called Battistello. Other early influences certainly include the Spanish artist Jusepe de Ribera, also residing in Naples. Contemporary documents place Stanzione in Rome from 1617 to 1618 and again around 1625. Initially he worked in a Caravaggesque mode well suited to the portraits and secular subject matter that dominate this early phase of his career. However, after 1617 a developing classicism is discernible in his paintings. The idealized forms and more decorative palette reflect the work of several Bolognese artists whose paintings Stanzione could have seen in Rome, principally Annibale Carracci, Domenichino, and Guido Reni. From this time onward religious subjects took up an ever greater portion of Stanzione's work, and he carried out numerous official commissions for the churches of Naples. His classicizing tendency was further strengthened around 1630 by contact with the paintings of Artemisia Gentileschi. The existence of a dated painting from 1658 puts into question de Dominici's assertion that Stanzione died in the plague of 1656. However, after 1655 no further mention of the artist is found in contemporary documents. Stanzione's principal student was Bernardo Cavallino.

2
Woman in Neapolitan Costume.   c.1635

Many ideas have been put forward to explain the unusual imagery of this painting, which depicts a young woman in an elaborately decorated costume holding a rooster in her left hand. The specificity of the details of costume and physiognomy suggests that this is a portrait of a particular individual. But whether she is a peasant woman in ceremonial garb or a young noblewoman in fanciful peasant costume is not understood. The inclusion of the rooster is surely intended to add a symbolic element to the composition, thus transforming a traditional likeness into an allegorical portrait or personification.

In Cesare Ripa's *Iconologia* (a sixteenth-century dictionary of symbolic imagery) we read that a woman holding a rooster in the left hand was a conventional symbol for jealousy. More commonly in northern painting one finds the motif of a man holding a rooster, perhaps a reference to cuckoldry. Thus this painting probably contains a yet undetermined allusion to the themes of betrayal and jealousy. Because the rooster is symbolic of Saint Peter's betrayal of Christ, it has also been suggested that the San Francisco picture was originally paired with a depiction of Saint Peter.

The painting seems to date from after 1630, at the end of Stanzione's Caravaggesque period. In addition, the signature reads *EQMAX* ('EQ' stands for *Eques*, signifying knighthood). Although it has not been verified that Stanzione was ever knighted, he employed this monogram after his second documented trip to Rome. The intensity of the light–dark contrasts throws the three-quarter-length figure into full relief. But this effect is tempered by the rich coloration and decorative nature of the costume, suggesting the influence of Artemisia Gentileschi.

LFO

oil on canvas
118.5 x 96.5 cm
Signed with monogram at lower left: *EQMAX*.
On loan from The Hispanic Society of America
L41.1.2

Provenance:
The Duke of Sutherland, Stafford House, London, by 1837 (his sale, London, Christie's, 8 February 1908, no. 100, as Spanish School, *A Peasant Woman*); Archer M. Huntington, New York; gift to The Hispanic Society of America, New York, 1941; loan to the de Young, 1941.

Literature:
G. F. Waagen, *Works of Art and Artists in England*, London, 1838, vol. 2, pp. 248–9; G. F. Waagen,

Treasures of Art in Great Britain, London, 1854, vol. 2, p. 65.

Exhibited:
Sarasota, Florida, The John and Mable Ringling Museum of Art, *Baroque Painters of Naples*, 1961, no. 9, repr.;
London, Royal Academy of Arts; Washington, DC, National Gallery of Art; Paris, Grand Palais; Turin, Palazzo Reale, *Painting in Naples, 1606–1705: From Caravaggio to Giordano*, 1982–83, no. 158, fig. 158, colour back cover;
Sarasota, Florida, The John and Mable Ringling Museum of Art, *Baroque Portraiture in Italy*, 1984–85, no. 70, repr.

Mattia Preti, called Il Cavaliere Calabrese
Italian, 1613–1699

Mattia Preti was born in Taverna, a town in Calabria then part of the kingdom of Naples. The young Preti joined his brother Gregorio, also a painter, in Rome around 1630. Between that time and 1653, when he moved to Naples, Preti travelled widely throughout northern Italy. During this period his initial Caravaggism, evident in both style and subject matter, was increasingly tempered by classicizing elements derived from Domenichino, Giovanni Lanfranco, Pier Francesco Mola, Pietro Testa and Guercino, among others. Most important in Preti's new, more sensuous palette was the influence of the Venetian High Renaissance, reflecting a general neo-Venetianism that characterized much Italian baroque painting at mid-century. In 1641 or 1642, while in Rome, Preti was created a knight in the Order of Saint John of Malta; thus he was called Il Cavaliere Calabrese, 'the knight from Calabria'. He arrived in Naples in 1653, during the great plague, which by 1656 had killed about one half of the city's population, including many of her artists. Preti quickly established himself as the leading painter in Naples, a position vigorously challenged by the younger Luca Giordano. These two artists created the Neapolitan high baroque. In 1656 Preti was commissioned by the city administrators to paint a series of frescos on the seven city gates — a bid to invoke divine protection from further ravages of the plague and from ensuing famine. Continuing to work in Naples until he returned briefly to Rome in 1660, and then moving permanently to Malta in 1661, Preti carried out numerous public and private commissions. He worked prodigiously on the island of Malta for forty years. His enormous output included important fresco cycles in Rome, Modena, Naples, Valmontone and Valletta, and his numerous altarpieces fill the churches of Malta, Naples and Taverna, his native town, where he sent many paintings. Preti died on 13 January 1699.

3
Saint John the Baptist Preaching. c.1665

Each of the four Gospels of the Bible tells the story of John the Baptist, who in the fifteenth year of the reign of Tiberius Caesar preached the coming of the Messiah. The story of John and his lineage is most completely told in the Gospel of Luke:

> The word of God came to John the son of Zechariah in the wilderness; and he went into all the regions about the Jordan, preaching a baptism of repentance for the forgiveness of sins. As it is written in the book of the words of Isaiah the prophet, 'The voice of one crying in the wilderness: Prepare the way of the Lord, Make his paths straight'. (3: 2–4)

The Gospel according to John the Evangelist recounts that when Jesus himself came from Galilee to be baptized by John in the waters of the Jordan, John said, 'Behold the Lamb of God, who takes away the sins of the world!' (John 1: 29). It is this phrase that appears in Latin on the banderole fluttering from the slender cross held by the Baptist: *EC[CE] AG[NUS] DEI.*

The figure of John the Baptist preaching, dressed in camel's-hair garb as noted in the Gospels, is among the most familiar images of Christian art. Popular during the Counter Reformation, it symbolized the Roman church's direct appeal to Catholics and Protestants alike to reaffirm their belief in the mysteries of the Catholic faith. The viewer of this painting is confronted by the gaze of a heroic, virile Saint John the Baptist, who is very different from the ascetic figure portrayed by El Greco (see cat. no. 1). The pose of Preti's Saint John creates a dynamic diagonal both across and into the pictorial space. The use of this kind of formal device to draw the spectator into the painted world is a principal characteristic of Italian baroque art. From Preti's most creative phase, this work embodies baroque power as the result of monumental scale and theatrical composition joined by dramatic lighting effects.   LFO

oil on canvas
219.0 x 170.0 cm
Museum purchase, Roscoe and Margaret Oakes
Income Fund and Kathryn Bache Miller Fund
1981.32

Provenance:
Private collection, Belgium; Galerie Heim, Paris; purchased by TFAMSF, 1981.

Exhibited:
New Haven, Yale University Art Gallery; Sarasota, Florida, The John and Mable Ringling Museum of Art; Kansas City, Missouri, Nelson-Atkins Museum of Art, *A Taste for Angels: Neapolitan Painting in North America, 1650–1750,* 1987–88, no. 5, colour repr.

Salvator Rosa
Italian, 1615–1673

Born in Naples, Salvator Rosa trained there with a succession of artists, including Francesco Fracanzano (his brother-in-law), Giovanni Lanfranco, Jusepe de Ribera and Aniello Falcone. Throughout his career these early influences coloured his art, particularly the battle scenes that, derived from Falcone, formed a recurrent motif in Rosa's oeuvre. In 1635 Rosa travelled to Rome, the pilgrimage site for all European artists, taking up residence there in 1638. In Rome he was exposed to a great diversity of styles, ranging from Caravaggesque realism to the emerging high baroque. He proved receptive to the stylistic novelties of other artists, such as Pieter van Laer, Herman van Swanevelt, Claude Lorrain and Nicolas Poussin. However, Rosa's interpretation of his various subjects was always personal. At the invitation of the Grand Duke of Tuscany, Rosa moved in 1640 to Florence, where he remained until 1649. In Florence, as in Rome, he took part in the literary life of the city, founding the Accademia del Percossi, a sophisticated group of writers and performers. In 1649 Rosa returned permanently to Rome, there participating in the yearly public exhibitions held in the portico of the Pantheon. His major artistic accomplishment was the creation of a new landscape type. Focused on nature's rugged formations, his compositions are infused with a moodiness and emotional energy echoing his petulant personality. Rosa's influence was considerable, inspiring a long line of followers from Marco Ricci to Thomas Cole, and peaking with the British adherents of romanticism.

4
Landscape with Travellers. c.1640

Dating from Rosa's first years in Rome, this painting is a vivid record of the artist's response to the newly popularized subjects of the Bambocciante, a group of artists who specialized in depictions of Italian genre or lowlife scenes, featuring beggars, peasants and brigands. The source of this coarse imagery was the work of Pieter van Laer, a Dutch artist working in Rome, who was nicknamed 'Bamboccio' (Clumsy Doll) because of a deformity. Such rustic subject matter found buyers among both the most discerning aristocratic collectors of the day and the wider public, exactly the audience that Rosa wished to attract.

In the present painting, Rosa emphasizes the picturesque aspects of his motley players: their coarse features, tattered clothes, amusing baggage and scruffy animals. Yet this humble entourage is realized in beautifully subtle harmonies of yellow, blue and brown, which tie the figures colouristically to the peaceful landscape behind them. The dark outcropping of rock, the silhouetted tree trunks, and the afternoon sky provide a poetic backdrop for the figures and reveal Rosa's awakening interest in the emotive potential of the landscape genre.

LFO

oil on canvas
143.5 x 170.2 cm
Museum purchase, Walter H. and Phyllis J. Shorenstein Foundation Fund and Roscoe and Margaret Oakes Income Fund
1987.10

Provenance:
Sir H. Carr Ibbetson, baronet, Denton Park, Yorkshire (inventory of 1760); *in situ* until sold with contents of house by Mrs Arthur Hill, July 1975; bought by Colnaghi, London and New York; Matthiesen Fine Art Ltd., London; purchased by TFAMSF, 1987.

Literature:
Lady Morgan, *Life and Times of Salvator Rosa*, London, 1824, vol. 2, p. 370; Federico Zeri, 'La percezione visiva dell'Italia e degli italiani nella storia della pittura', in *Storia d'Italia*, Turin, 1976, vol. 6, fig. 71; Luigi Salerno, *Pittori di paesaggio del seicento a Roma*, Rome, 1977–80, vol. 2, p. 547, fig. 87.5.

Exhibited:
London, *The Somerset House Art Treasures Exhibition*, 1979, p. 43, pl. 3;
London, Matthiesen Fine Art Ltd., *Important Italian Baroque Painting, 1600–1700*, 1981, no. 10, colour repr.;
London, Royal Academy of Arts; Washington, DC, National Gallery of Art, *Painting in Naples, 1606–1705: From Caravaggio to Giordano*, 1982–83, no. 132, repr.;
New York, Richard L. Feigen & Co., *Landscape Painting in Rome, 1595–1675*, 1985, no. 44, repr.

Giovanni Battista Gaulli, called Il Baciccio
Italian, 1639–1709

It is believed that Gaulli, known as Baciccio (the Genoese nickname for Giovanni Battista), left his native Genoa after his entire family perished, presumably in the plague of 1657. At that time he moved permanently to Rome. During the decade of the 1660s he established himself as one of the leading artists working in the Eternal City, most particularly as the result of the favour of the illustrious sculptor Gian Lorenzo Bernini. Baciccio became a member of the Academy of Saint Luke in 1662 and held several offices in that body. Through Bernini's recommendation he was chosen over such competitors as Carlo Maratta, Giacento Brandi and Ciro Ferri to execute the decorative cycle for the interior of the church of Il Gesù, the recently completed mother church of the Jesuit order. Begun in 1676, the nave vault fresco, *The Triumph of the Name of Jesus*, was unveiled on New Year's Eve of 1679. In this work, universally considered the culmination of baroque illusionistic ceiling painting, Baciccio masterfully orchestrated painting and sculptural details within the architectural context. He created a tumultuous scene of figures that seem to hover over or tumble into the viewer's space. Baciccio continued to work in Il Gesù until 1685, frescoing nave, dome, pendentives, apse and transept vaults. The total ensemble is one of the glories of the Counter Reformation. Stylistically, Baciccio's works reveal the lasting influence of his Genoese heritage. His early exposure to fellow Genoese artists, including Valerio Castello and Giovanni Benedetto Castiglione, is evident in his vibrant colouring, activated drapery and fluid figural lines. In addition, he employed the energetic brushstroke introduced to Genoa in the 1620s by the Flemish artist Anthony van Dyck. In his later works Baciccio set aside the flamboyant rhythms and colours of the high baroque, conceding to the ascendancy of late baroque classicism.

5
The Adoration of the Lamb.   c.1680
(*modello* for the apse fresco in Il Gesù, Rome)

In 1679, with the completion of the fresco on the nave vault of Il Gesù, Gian Paolo Oliva, the Father-General of the Society of Jesus, wished to engage Baciccio to fresco the apse. To this end he sought the permission and assistance of Ranuccio Il Farnese, Duke of Parma, whose family had initially supported the building of Il Gesù. Permission was quickly granted; thus, the San Francisco painting must date from around that time.

The completion of the apse fresco was celebrated in 1683 on 30 July, the feastday of Saint Ignatius. The present work is a vibrant oil sketch, or *modello* — Baciccio's early conception for the apse fresco. In the completed fresco itself and in the San Francisco painting, Christ is symbolized by the sacrificial lamb resting on a book on the altar at the centre of the scene. Encircling the lamb is a host of heavenly figures; each is marvellously suggested with loose, broad brushstrokes. The source of this painting's iconography is the mystical visions of Saint John the Evangelist as revealed in the biblical book of Revelation; here the lamb of God lies on the book with its seven seals, which symbolize the seven revelations of the Evangelist.

LFO

oil on canvas
64.5 x 113.0 cm (oval)
Gift of the M. H. de Young Endowment Fund
54680

Provenance:
Michel Angelo Lucioni, Rome, by January 1877 (according to label pasted on back of canvas); possibly Pope Pius IX, The Vatican, 1877; J. Gollober, San Francisco; I. Wollenberg, San Francisco; purchased by de Young, 1935 (as by Sebastiano Conca).

Literature:
Ebria Feinblatt, 'Jesuit Ceiling Decoration', *Art Quarterly* 10 (Summer 1947), p. 253 n. 4, fig. 12; Robert Enggass, *The Painting of Baciccio*, University

Park, Pennsylvania, 1964, pp. 67, 157, 178, fig. 86; Dieter Graf, 'Giovanni Battista Gaullis Ölskizzen im Kunstmuseum Düsseldorf', *Pantheon* 31 (April–June 1973), pp. 167–71, fig. 13.

Exhibited:
San Francisco, CPLH, *Italian Baroque Painting*, 1941, no. 3, fig. 3; Dayton Art Institute; Sarasota, Florida, The John and Mable Ringling Museum of Art; Hartford, Connecticut, The Wadsworth Atheneum, *Genoese Masters: Cambiaso to Magnasco*, 1962–63, no. 35, repr.; The Detroit Institute of Arts, *Art in Italy, 1600–1700*, 1965, no. 49, repr.; The Denver Art Museum, *Baroque Art: Era of Elegance*, 1971, p. 28, repr. p. 29.

Gaspare Giovanni Traversi
Italian, 1722/1724–1770

Gaspare Giovanni Traversi trained in his native city of Naples with Francesco Solimena. The stylistic influence of Solimena's florid late baroque idiom can be seen in Traversi's early series of scenes from the life of the Virgin, painted in 1749 for the church of Santa Maria dell'Aiuto in Naples. After Solimena's death in 1747 Traversi seems to have been attracted to the works of another of his teacher's students, fellow Neapolitan Francesco de Mura. Before Traversi moved to Rome, where he is recorded as residing from 1755 until his death in 1770, his style had begun to change, tempered by the dark realism of the Spanish artist Jusepe de Ribera and the Neapolitan works of Caravaggio. However, Traversi's style changed markedly after his arrival in Rome, where he was immediately struck by the narrative power, realism and lighter tonality of the paintings from Caravaggio's Roman period. The early works of Caravaggio, and those of his early followers, including Bartolommeo Manfredi, Valentin de Boulogne and Gerrit van Honthorst, provided Traversi with a style and subject matter more sympathetic to his own taste than was the decorative model of Solimena. Traversi's best genre scenes capture the rich flavour of everyday life, combining elements of seventeenth-century Caravaggesque realism with the colouristic palette and biting social satire typical of genre painters of the eighteenth century.

6
The Fortune Teller. c.1760

oil on canvas
68.0 x 94.6 cm
Gift of Collis P. Huntington
8549

Provenance:
Galerie Sedelmeyer, Paris (as possibly by Piazzetta); Collis P. Huntington, New York, by 1899; gift to the de Young, 1899.

Literature:
Alfred Moir, *The Italian Followers of Caravaggio*, Cambridge, Mass., 1967, vol. 1, p. 181; vol. 2, pp. 38, 111, fig. 230; *Civiltà del 1700 a Napoli, 1734–1799*, Naples, 1979, p. 222, fig. 109a; Ferdinando Bologna, *Gaspare Traversi nell illuminismo europeo*, Naples, 1980, pp. 51–3, 76 n. 97, fig. 33.

7
The Merry Company.   c.1760

Typical of the work of Traversi, these two paintings were conceived as a pair. They are an eighteenth-century adaptation of the half-length genre picture, not invented by Caravaggio but popularized by him and his followers in Rome around the year 1600. The San Francisco *Fortune Teller* specifically reflects Caravaggio's two versions of the same subject (Paris, Musée du Louvre; Rome, Museo Capitolino).

The realism of the figures in such Caravaggesque paintings is heightened by several formal means, including the great attention paid to the details and surface textures of costume and physiognomy. Most important, the characters appear unidealized, seemingly drawn directly from the world around the artist. The almost life-size figures are pushed close to the pictorial surface, so that their forms are partially cut off by the edge of the picture. They seem to extend into our space, and, because of their proximity to us, we become not just onlookers but actual participants in the scene. In *The Merry Company*, this effect is further enhanced by the direct eye contact established by the old man, who doffs his hat at us from within the picture. Traversi's approach is less realistic than Caravaggio's, as the eighteenth-century artist pays less attention to precise description of details. Instead, he emphasizes the physical and social coarseness of his figures, their wrinkled faces and gnarled hands accentuated almost to the grotesque. He also employs a dry brush over a dark ground, which creates a patchiness in the skin and drapery passages. In this technique, and in his interpretation of the genre figures, Traversi is closely aligned with other eighteenth-century Italian artists, such as Giacomo Ceruti and Giovanni Battista Piazzetta, who combine a certain earthiness of subject matter with the refined pastel coloration of the rococo.

LFO

oil on canvas
68.6 x 94.3 cm
Gift of Collis P. Huntington
8550

Provenance:
Same as for *The Fortune Teller.*

Literature:
Civiltà del 1700 a Napoli, 1734–1799, Naples, 1979, p. 222, fig. 109b; Ferdinando Bologna, *Gaspare Traversi nell illuminismo europeo,* Naples, 1980, pp. 53, 60, 76 n. 97, 84–5, fig. 40.

Dutch and Flemish Paintings

Frans Hals
Dutch, 1582/1583–1666

Recent research in the Antwerp civic archives has established that Frans Hals must have been born there about 1582–83, before his parents left for Haarlem in 1585, when Antwerp was retaken by the Spanish. The role of Hals's teacher has been ascribed to the Haarlem artist-biographer Karel van Mander; however, nothing of that artist's dry mannerism is discernible in Hals's works. Entering the painters' guild of Haarlem in 1610, Hals established his reputation as a superb portraitist with the 1616 group portrait *The Banquet of the Officers of the Saint George Civic Guard* (Haarlem, Frans Halsmuseum). His portraits depict prosperous individuals and civic groups of Haarlem and other Dutch cities, as well as prominent thinkers of the day, such as René Descartes, whose portrait Hals painted in 1649. Hals was the leading artistic personality in Haarlem, attracting many students including Adriaen Brouwer, Judith Leyster and Philips Wouwermans. However, not until the mid-nineteenth century were Hals's originality and technical skill fully recognized. In fact, during his later years, mounting debts forced him to apply to the city of Haarlem for a small annual pension to allow him to meet even his modest living expenses.

8
Portrait of a Gentleman in White. *c.1637*

The recent cleaning of the *Gentleman in White* has enhanced the brilliance of the painting's spontaneous brushwork. The deftness with which the facial planes have been constructed is now more apparent, as subtleties of tonal gradation join with dashes of purer colour to suggest the form and vitality of the skin passages. In this specific combination of refinement and boldness, the San Francisco painting is closely related to the signed and dated *Portrait of a Man* of 1637 (Stuttgart, Staatsgalerie). Both portraits approach the representation of form, outline and costume in a similar manner. For example, in each, the shoulder is outlined with short zigzag brushstrokes, which activate the contours with little respect for the realities of the costume itself. Independent of the image they re-create, such brisk individual strokes exist as abstract patterns floating on the pictorial surface.

Hals does not, however, allow the freedom with which the paint is applied in the drapery passages to take precedence over the description of the facial features. Rendered with much tighter brushstrokes, the face is brought to life by a warmer coloration. In this portrait the vigour of the brushwork suggests the personality of the sitter, who appears arrogant and strong willed.

The contrast between the staccato brushwork of the costume, which in patches is more mechanical than one would expect from Hals, and the fluidity of the facial planes, coupled with the somewhat awkward placement of the projecting elbow, has led some scholars to speculate that this portrait is not by the master himself. Yet the personality of the sitter is placed before us with such consummate skill that the image is as compelling psychologically as it is pictorially. Although the authorship is still unresolved, the beauty and vitality of the portrait reward the viewer's attention.

LFO

oil on canvas
68.8 x 58.8 cm
Roscoe and Margaret Oakes Collection
75.2.5

Provenance:
Arthur J. Sulley, London, by 1921; M. Knoedler & Co., New York, 1922–25; Mrs Samuel S. Rotan, Philadelphia, 1925–55; Frederick Mont, New York; Roscoe and Margaret Oakes, San Francisco; gift to TFAMSF, 1975.

Literature:
Wilhelm R. Valentiner, *Frans Hals (Klassiker der Kunst)*, Stuttgart and Berlin, 1921, p. 322, repr. p. 283; Seymour Slive, *Frans Hals*, London, 1970, vol. 3, no. D52, fig. 173; Claus Grimm and E. C. Montagni, *L'opera completa di Frans Hals*, Milan, 1974, no. 101, repr.; Christopher Wright, *The Art of the Forger*, New York, 1985, pp. 101, 133–4, 156; Claus Grimm, *Frans Hals: The Complete Work*, New York, 1989, pp. 138–9, 184, 193, 282, no. 84, colour pl. 38, 61 (detail).

Anthony van Dyck
Flemish, 1599–1641

The records of the Antwerp Guild of Saint Luke first mention Anthony van Dyck, who was born in that city in 1599, as an apprentice of Hendrick van Balen in 1609. By 1618 van Dyck was received by the guild as an independent master. Prior to that time he had established contact with the older Peter Paul Rubens. The scanty contemporary evidence suggests a changing collaborative relationship between the two artists, for van Dyck would move from the position of a gifted apprentice to that of the most important member of Rubens's large studio. In the autumn of 1620 van Dyck is first recorded in England, at the court of James I. Returning briefly to Antwerp in 1624, he then travelled to Italy, visiting Genoa, Venice, Florence, Rome and Palermo before arriving back in Antwerp by the beginning of 1628. The effect of Venetian colourism, particularly as seen in the works of Titian, reinforced lessons learned from Rubens; van Dyck remained a brilliant colourist throughout his career. Working in Antwerp until 1632, he then returned to England at the invitation of Charles I, who knighted him that year. Except for brief visits to the Continent, van Dyck would spend the rest of his life in England, where he died at the age of forty-two. An accomplished history painter, he is best known today as a portraitist. In addition to his consummate technical skill, his ability to capture the facial features of his portrait subjects and to characterize their social status soon made him much sought after by Europe's aristocracy. His portraits from the first Genoese period and later, which were initially based on the Italian portraits of Rubens, created the vocabulary of aristocratic portraiture that remained pre-eminent until the nineteenth century and that helped to shape England's great portrait tradition.

9
Marie Claire de Croy, Duchesse d'Havré, and Child.   1634

The traditional identification of the sitter in this portrait as Marie Claire de Croy, who married her cousin Charles Philippe Alexandre de Croy, Duke of Havré, is based on an inscription found on an engraved portrait of Marie Claire by Conrad Woumans. That likeness is part of a series of engraved portraits of contemporary people entitled *Iconographie*, which is designed after drawings and oil sketches by van Dyck. Although it is possible to see a certain likeness of facial features and similarity of costume in the painting and engraving, the identification of the young woman in the San Francisco picture as Marie Claire de Croy is far from secure.

As indicated by the contemporaneous inscription, this life-size double portrait dates from 1634, when van Dyck was again in Flanders. He has positioned the woman deep in the pictorial space. She seems to tower over us, her downward stare riveting us in place. Her sheer physical size and attenuated proportions allude to her elevated social status, which is explicitly defined by her opulent dress and the palatial backdrop. The stiff formality of the pose of the mother, accentuated by the vertical lines of her costume, is countered by the active pose and colourful, if formal, dress of the child at her side. The sex of this child has been the subject of conjecture; however, such dress was not uncommon for little boys of the aristocracy at that time. More important, the full skill of the artist is apparent in the rendering of the luminous skin passages and the shimmering garb of the child. The nervous refinement of van Dyck's brushwork activates the outlines of the figure and brings the entire composition to life.

LFO

oil on canvas
208.9 x 124.0 cm
Inscribed at lower left: *CAVALo A VAN DYCK.F.A. 1634*
Roscoe and Margaret Oakes Collection
58.43

Provenance:
Ayscough Fawkes, Farnley Hall, Otley, Yorkshire, by 1886; T. C. Farrer, London, sold by 1887; to Hamilton McKay Twombly, New York, 1887; to Ruth Vanderbilt Twombly, New York (her sale, New York, Parke Bernet, 8 January 1955, no. 393, as *The Duchess of Arenberg and Child*); purchased by David Koetser,

New York; to Roscoe and Margaret Oakes, San Francisco, 1955; gift to the de Young, 1958.

Literature:
Michael Jaffé, 'Van Dyck Portraits in the de Young Museum and Elsewhere', *Art Quarterly* 28, nos 1–2 (1965), pp. 41–2, 44, 45, fig. 2, p. 53; Erik Larsen, *L'opera completa di Van Dyck, 1626–1641*, Milan, 1980, vol. 2, no. 784, fig. 784, and colour pl. XXXIX, XL (detail); Erik Larsen, *The Paintings of Anthony van Dyck*, Freren, 1988, vol. 1, p. 343, fig. 372; vol. 2, no. 822.

$\mathcal{OS}$alomon van Ruysdael

Dutch, 1600/1603–1670

Born Salomon de Gooyer (or Goyer) in Naarden in Gooiland, the artist was received into the Haarlem guild in 1623 under that name. Subsequently, however, he took the name Ruysdael (sometimes signed *Ruyesdael*), derived from Castle Ruisdael (Ruis-schendaal), a landmark near his father's hometown. In 1628, two years after his first extant dated painting, Salomon is already noted as an accomplished landscapist in the writings of the Haarlem chronicler Samuel van Ampzig. Salomon would spend his entire artistic career in Haarlem, the site of many early innovations in the development of Dutch naturalistic landscape painting. Of particular importance to his early style was the work of Esaias van de Velde, who had worked in Haarlem from 1609 to 1618. Van de Velde's unaffected views of typically Dutch terrain formed the basis of the work of Ruysdael, Jan van Goyen (who had been a pupil of van de Velde) and Pieter de Molijn (whose own influence is discernible in Salomon's work). Together these three younger artists were the principal exponents of Dutch tonal landscape painting. Not until the 1640s did the monochromatic colour scheme characteristic of this phase give way to a more colourful and compositionally classical period, from which date Ruysdael's best works. Settling on river scenery as his primary subject, Salomon varied his compositions with great skill, focusing on the ways that light and atmosphere changed and qualified the natural components of his paintings: land, water and foliage, all placed beneath a cloud-filled sky. Ruysdael, a Mennonite, died in 1670 and was buried in Saint Bavo's Church in his adopted Haarlem. He was the uncle of the more famous Jacob van Ruisdael and the father of Jacob Salomonsz. van Ruysdael, who was also a landscape artist.

10

River View of Nijmegen with the Valkhof. 1648

With Dutch independence from Catholic Hapsburg Spain, initiated in 1609 by the Twelve-Years' Truce, came a new sense of national pride and an interest in the political history of Dutch towns and landmarks. Among the most ancient and historically significant cities was Nijmegen, the capital of Gelderland. Situated near the German border on five low hills overlooking the River Waal, one of the main tributaries of the Rhine, Nijmegen was a site of strategic importance, held consecutively by Batavians, Romans, Charlemagne, the Holy Roman Empire and, in the seventeenth century, by the Dutch republic. Nijmegen was recorded by Tacitus as the seat of the Batavian revolt, which people in the seventeenth century saw as the ancient precedent for the political struggle of the modern Dutch nation against the Spanish. As such, the city was the subject of much attention, in both the writings of historians and the work of artists, such as Rembrandt and a succession of landscapists, including Aelbert Cuyp, Jan van Goyen and Salomon van Ruysdael.

The San Francisco composition focuses on the massive tower of the Valkhof (Falcon Court), which rises above the river. The fortress had originally been constructed by Charlemagne beginning in 777; it was almost completely rebuilt by Frederick Barbarossa after 1155.

Introducing a new phase in Ruysdael's career, *River View of Nijmegen with the Valkhof* moves away from the monochromatic tonalities typical of Dutch landscape painting in the previous decades. Instead, it is characterized by a novel heightened palette, coupled with a greater sense of form. Always interested in atmospheric effects, Ruysdael depicts dramatic cloud formations, which echo and augment the imposing castle architecture. LFO

oil on canvas
104.0 x 143.8 cm
Signed and dated on ferry: *S V Ruysdael 1648*
Gift of the Samuel H. Kress Foundation
61.44.36

Provenance:
Count Stanislaus Potocki, Paris (his sale, Paris, Galerie Georges Petit, 8 May 1885, no. 47); bought by Petitpont; John Nicholson Gallery, New York; Samuel H. Kress Foundation, New York, 1952; gift to the de Young, 1961.

Literature:
Wolfgang Stechow, *Salomon van Ruysdael*, Berlin, 1938, no. 354; Wolfgang Stechow, *Dutch Landscape Painting of the Seventeenth Century*, London, 1966, p. 56, fig. 100; Wolfgang Stechow, *Salomon van Ruysdael*, 2nd ed., Berlin, 1975, no. 354, fig. 35, pl. 26; Colin Eisler, *Paintings from the Samuel H. Kress Collection: European Schools Excluding Italian*, Oxford, 1977, pp. 145–6, fig. 131.

Exhibited:
New Brunswick, New Jersey, The Jane Vorhees Zimmerli Art Museum, Rutgers University, *Haarlem: The Seventeenth Century*, 1983, no. 107, repr. p. 122.

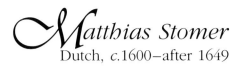

Matthias Stomer
Dutch, c.1600–after 1649

Few seventeenth-century documents comment on Matthias Stomer's life or works. Those contemporary sources that do exist consistently give the artist's name as 'Stom', although he is traditionally referred to as 'Stomer'. A reference of 1630–32 records that '*Matteo Stom, fiamengo pittore, di anni 30* [Matthias Stom, Flemish painter, thirty years old]' was living in the parish of San Nicola in Arcione in Rome. From this it can be deduced that Stomer was a northern artist, who, born around 1600, had established himself in the Eternal City by 1630. His stylistic indebtedness to the art of both the Utrecht Caravaggists (Gerrit van Honthorst, Dirck van Baburen and Hendrick ter Brugghen) and various Antwerp artists suggests that he was born and had trained in southern Holland. Later documents, such as the 1648 inventory of the collection of Don Antonio Ruffo, Duke of Messina, place Stomer in Sicily, where he seems to have moved permanently sometime after 1632, following a stay of undetermined length in Naples. The hallmark of Stomer's art is his personal interpretation of the Caravaggesque idiom. This stylistic vocabulary, learned initially from the northern followers of Caravaggio and then experienced at first hand in Rome, was further enhanced by Stomer's access to the later works of Caravaggio decorating churches in Naples and Sicily. Of Stomer's surviving works only the *Saint Isidore Agricola* of 1641, formerly in the church of Caccamo near Palermo, is securely dated. Consequently, the chronology of his paintings has been established largely on the basis of their internal evidence.

11
The Calling of Saint Matthew.   c.1629

Based on Caravaggio's painting of the same subject, which had been executed some thirty years earlier for the church of San Luigi dei Francesi in Rome, Stomer's *Calling of Saint Matthew* is a *tour de force* of baroque internalized drama and compositional sophistication. In addition to reversing the original composition, Stomer employs a number of formal devices popularized by Caravaggio: sharp light–dark contrasts, which create a theatrical play of light across the forms; careful attention to realistic detail and surface textures; and, most important, the interpretation of sacred Christian events in terms of everyday life, with ordinary people representing the most holy personages. These almost life-size figures are posed in a shallow stagelike space, close to the picture plane. This placement, coupled with the intrusion of the frame on the figures, accentuates the monumentality of the human forms, their physical weight echoing the emotional gravity of the event. Although no supporting documentary evidence has come to light, the religious subject matter and the sheer scale of the San Francisco painting suggest that it was done on commission for a church. Similarly, the closeness of Stomer's composition to Caravaggio's original conception argues for a date shortly after Stomer's arrival in the Eternal City, when Caravaggio's Roman paintings made their freshest and most vivid impression on him.

The painting illustrates the moment when Christ challenges the Roman tax collector Levi to forsake the privileges of his imperial post and to 'Follow me' (Luke 5: 27–8). Levi, the man seated at the far right, will indeed follow Jesus' lead and will thereafter be known as the apostle Matthew. The psychological tie between Jesus and Levi, to which the attending figures seem largely oblivious, is reinforced by the coloration of their two costumes, in which similar shades of red and blue frame the scene like parentheses and redirect attention to the centre of the figural group. There the grouping of hands, book and scales is a virtuoso display of convincing spatial effects.

LFO

oil on canvas
175.0 x 224.0 cm
Museum purchase, Roscoe and Margaret Oakes
Income Fund
1986.27

Provenance:
Possibly Don Giuseppe Branciforti, Principe di Butera, Mazzerino, Sicily (inventory of 1675); Lord James Butler, Drumcondra Castle, Ireland, by 1872; Albright-Knox Art Gallery, Buffalo, NY (as by circle of Honthorst); sale, New York, Christie's, 18 June 1982, no. 114 (as by Stomer); bought by Matthiesen Fine Art, Ltd., London; purchased by TFAMSF, 1986.

Literature:
Benedict Nicolson, *Caravaggism in Europe*, 2nd ed., Turin, 1989, vol. 1, p. 185; vol. 2, no. 1557, repr.

Exhibited:
Dublin, *Art, Industries, and Manufactures, and Loan Museum of Works of Art*, 1872, no. 31 (as *Calling of Levi* by Caravaggio);
London, Matthiesen Fine Art Ltd., *Around 1610: The Onset of the Baroque*, 1985, no. 31, colour repr.;
Utrecht, Centraal Museum; Braunschweig, Herzog Anton Ulrich-Museum, *Holländische Malerei in neuem Licht: Hendrick ter Brugghen und seine Zeitgenossen*, 1986–87, no. 75, colour repr.

Rembrandt Harmensz. van Rijn

Dutch, 1606–1669

Rembrandt was born in Leiden and began his training in that city with the obscure painter Jacob van Swanenburgh. He then became an apprentice in the Amsterdam studio of Pieter Lastman, who instilled in the younger artist a lifelong preference for history painting. Returning briefly to Leiden, Rembrandt worked there in association with Jan Lievens before moving permanently, in late 1631, to Amsterdam, where he quickly established his reputation as a portraitist. The 1630s was a particularly prosperous decade, during which Rembrandt married Saskia van Uylenburgh, the wealthy niece of the art dealer Hendrick Uylenburgh. While always returning to the human figure as his primary subject, during the 1640s Rembrandt explored the formal properties and emotional potential of the landscape genre. At this time he also experimented with etching, a graphic medium he frequently used in combination with drypoint to achieve a richness of effect. In general, the decade of the 1640s was marked by reversals of both a personal and a professional nature, most notably Saskia's death in 1642, which had been preceded by the deaths of all but one of their four children. During this period Rembrandt developed a broader manner of execution realized in a darker palette, which became more exaggerated in later years. This quality made his portraits less popular with clients who sought precisely rendered detail of face and costume. However, the style was well suited to the introspective portraits and biblical subjects that fascinated the artist. He continued to receive important commissions, including the fabled *Night Watch* of 1642 (Amsterdam, Rijksmuseum) and the rejected *Conspiracy of the Batavians* (Stockholm, National-museum), commissioned in 1661 for the Amsterdam Town Hall. He also worked for wealthy private patrons, such as Jan Six and Antonio Ruffo of Sicily. A genius of extraordinary technical talent and perception, Rembrandt influenced a large number of students and followers, including Gerard Dou, Carel and Barendt Fabritius, Nicolaes Maes and Aert de Gelder.

12
Joris de Caulerij. 1632

Much has come to light regarding the life and social circumstances of Joris de Caulerij, the sitter in this outstanding portrait. Of particular importance is the 1 July 1654 document in which de Caulerij willed to his heirs this painting by Rembrandt and other portraits of himself and his wife, Maria de la Samme (or Somme). Untraced works by Jan Lievens and Anthony van Dyck are also mentioned in addition to a portrait of Joris by Moyses van Uyttenbroeck, a work that can possibly be identified as that in the collection of H. M. W. van der Wijck in Doorn. A second portrait by Rembrandt, representing de Caulerij's eldest son, Jacob, is itemized in Joris's will of 1661.

In the San Francisco painting Joris is represented as a militiaman of The Hague wearing the garb of the *kloveniersgilde* (harquebusiers' guild); in his hand he holds a *roer* (a small musket). Confusion surrounding the identification of this object, stemming from the misinterpretation of the word *roer*, which can also mean 'rudder', has been unequivocally laid to rest. In addition to the will of 1654, a series of contemporary documents relates a long list of de Caulerij's naval accomplishments. They include distinguished service in the first Dutch–English War (1652–54) and the sea war with Sweden (1658–59). He saw action at the 1656 Siege of Danzig and at the Battle of the Sont in 1658. De Caulerij died in Denmark in 1661.

The talents of the young Rembrandt probably came to de Caulerij's attention when the artist was working in The Hague for Frederick Hendrick. Contemporary with Rembrandt's arrival in Amsterdam, this signed and dated portrait of 1632 makes it immediately apparent why he displaced Amsterdam's leading portraitists, Thomas de Keyser and Nicolaes Elias. The San Francisco painting demonstrates Rembrandt's early mastery of the portrait idiom, which combines the sympathetic characterization of the sitter with striking three-dimensionality and atmospheric effects.

LFO

oil on canvas transferred to panel
102.5 x 83.8 cm
Signed and dated at lower right: *RHL* (in monogram)
van Ryn/1632
Roscoe and Margaret Oakes Collection
66.31

Provenance:
Joris de Caulerij, The Hague, 1632–61; to Josina de
Caulerij, The Hague, 1661–1712; to Sara de Caulerij,
The Hague, 1712–22; to George van der Poel, The
Hague, 1722–50; Stortenbeker, The Hague, 1867; J. H.
J. Quarles van Ufford, The Hague, before 1881–90; A.
Preyer, Amsterdam, 1890; Charles T. Yerkes, Chicago,
1890 (his sale, New York, American Art Galleries, 7
April 1910, no. 115); bought by Jacques Seligmann,
Paris and New York, 1910; G. Rasmussen, Chicago,
1924; John Levy Galleries, New York, 1937; to Edwin
D. Levinson, New York, 1937–54; to Edna Levinson
(Mrs M. M. Ripin) and Evelyn Levinson (Mrs E. A.
Stein), New York, 1954–55; Knoedler & Co., New
York, 1955 (on consignment from the Levinson estate
through Julius H. Weitzner, Inc.); to Roscoe and
Margaret Oakes, San Francisco, 1955; gift to the de
Young, 1966.

Literature:
Wilhelm R. Valentiner, *Rembrandt (Klassiker der
Kunst)*, Stuttgart and Leipzig, 1909, p. 85, repr., p. 552;
Horst Gerson, *Rembrandt Paintings*, Amsterdam, 1968,
pp. 48, 208, 266, 494, no. 124, repr.; Abraham Bredius,
The Paintings of Rembrandt, 3rd ed., rev. by Horst
Gerson, London, 1969, pp. 145, 562, no. 170, repr.;
Christopher Brown, *Rembrandt: The Complete
Paintings*, London and New York, 1980, vol. 1, no. 87,
repr.; Abraham Bredius, 'De Portretten van Joris de
Caullery', *Oud-Holland* 11 (1983), pp. 127–8; Gary
Schwartz, *Rembrandt: His Life, His Paintings*, New
York, 1985, no. 62; *A Corpus of Rembrandt Paintings*,
vol. 2, *1631–1634*, Boston, 1986, pp. 7–8, 26, 92,
106, 199–205, no. A53, repr.

Exhibited:
New York World's Fair, *Masterpieces of Art*, 1940,
no. 86;
The Hague, Mauritshuis; San Francisco, TFAMSF, *Great
Dutch Paintings from America*, 1990–91, no. 50,
colour repr.

Michael Sweerts
Flemish, 1618–1664

Little is known about Michael Sweerts's early years, except that he was baptized at the church of Saint Nicholas in Brussels in 1618, the son of a Catholic linen merchant. Further documentation appears in 1646 when he is recorded in Rome amid the resident community of northern artists, residing in the Via Margutta. Nothing is known about his early training or travels, but his Roman works develop from the tradition of the Bambocciante, followers of the Dutch artist Pieter van Laer. Sweerts is best known for his depictions of Italian peasants; however, unlike the works of the other Bambocciante, his paintings exhibit an inner balance and harmony, which imbue the peasant figures with classical form and dignity. In spite of his penchant for lowlife street scenes, Sweerts also painted interior genre scenes, single figures and formal portraits, and was an accomplished etcher. A member of the Academy of Saint Luke, he was in Rome until at least 1652, subsequently returning to the Low Countries. In Brussels by 1656, he established a drawing academy, a relatively rare institution in northern Europe and probably based on Italian prototypes. Although Flemish by birth, Sweerts possessed an artistic style that is more Dutch in character. Thus it is not surprising to learn that he had settled in Amsterdam prior to 1661. It was from that city that he departed for the Far East as a lay brother in the company of a French missionary. He is later recorded as a visitor at a Portuguese Jesuit mission in India, dying in Goa in 1664.

13
Portrait of a Youth.   c.1655–61

While not unique in the artist's oeuvre (see, for example, the comparable works in The Wadsworth Atheneum, Hartford, Connecticut and Leicester Art Gallery, Leicester, England), this wistful depiction of a youth is certainly one of Sweerts's masterpieces. Quiet, understated and tangible, this image is the essence of northern baroque illusionism. The immediacy of the figure, tightly cropped and pushed close to the picture plane, creates an air of intense intimacy. The liquid eyes, the moist, parted lips, and the turn of the head all suggest that the figure has just reacted to some distraction 'off-camera'. This sense of movement is echoed in the recurring curvilinear accents in the collar and tendrils of hair. These formal elements join to produce a composition charged with life, an energy inherent in the forms themselves and not reliant on actual gesture or movement.

Although no direct contact can be established, the intimacy of Sweerts's vision and the transitory nature of his portrait-like works find their closest parallel in the contemporary paintings of Johannes Vermeer. Of particular relevance are Vermeer's single figures, such as the *Head of a Girl*, c.1660 (The Hague, Mauritshuis). The specifically Dutch quality of the group of paintings to which the San Francisco picture belongs has led to the assumption that they date from Sweerts's Amsterdam period, that is, from about 1660.

LFO

oil on canvas
39.4 x 34.8 cm
Roscoe and Margaret Oakes Collection
66.9

Provenance:
Captain James Fraser, mid-eighteenth century; by family descent to Mrs Ann Warner; to Mrs Elizabeth Warner; to A. Dawes; to A. E. Dawes (his sale, London, Sotheby's, 3 March 1965, no. 94); to Julius H. Weitzner, Inc., London; Roscoe and Margaret Oakes, San Francisco, 1965; gift to the de Young, 1966.

Literature:
Ben Broos, *Great Dutch Paintings from America*, exh. cat., The Hague, 1990, p. 439, fig. 1.

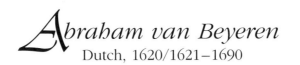

Abraham van Beyeren
Dutch, 1620/1621–1690

Born in The Hague, Abraham van Beyeren, the eldest son of a glass-maker, seems to have resided in his native city, except for a brief sojourn in Leiden, until about 1657. At that time he moved to Delft and thereafter moved repeatedly, returning to The Hague by 1663, living in Amsterdam from 1669 to 1674, in Alkmaar from 1674 to 1678, then in Gouda, and finally in Overschie from 1678 until his death in 1690. Van Beyeren was one of the founding members of the Confreria Pictura organized in The Hague in 1656 to replace the unsuccessful local chapter of the artists' guild, to which he had belonged since 1640. He also joined the painters' guild in Delft in 1657. Married in 1639, he remarried in 1647 after the death of his first wife. His second marriage was to the daughter of the portrait painter Crispiaen van der Quebon. Van Beyeren's early works were still-life paintings of fish. This concentration led to the belief that he was influenced by the painter of fish still lifes Pieter de Putter, who specialized in the same subject matter and who was the husband of van Beyeren's second wife's aunt. Important stylistic influences certainly come from works by Jan Davidsz. de Heem and Jacques de Claeuw. Not confining himself to any one subject, van Beyeren created a variety of subject matter, perhaps always searching for a broader clientele. Although he painted seascapes, fish still lifes and flowerpieces, he is best known for his *pronk* (banquet) still lifes and is deservedly considered one of the most talented Dutch still-life painters of the second half of the seventeenth century.

14
Still Life. 1666

Works such as the San Francisco painting illustrate van Beyeren's response to the decorative approach of Jan Davidsz. de Heem, which in turn reveals the influence of the Flemish still-life tradition. In the banquet scenes of these two artists, the love of opulence is manifest not only in the abundance and complexity of the objects represented but also in the grandiose architectural settings and the heavy curtains draped swaglike behind the still-life groupings, all of which is augmented by a view into a landscape beyond a laden table. These elements combine to create an image of monumental conception and pictorial richness. The vividness of colour that van Beyeren employs is also reminiscent of the Flemish approach and adds verve to his best works. Textural differentiation is further heightened by the use of a very dry brush, allowing the artist to achieve a rich chalky effect, suggestive of the pastel medium; in the present work this technique may be seen in the drapery passages of the heavy velvet table covering. It is in this broader technique that van Beyeren seems to have been influenced by the paintings of Jacques de Claeuw.

As is typical of van Beyeren's work, in this picture there are several individual objects, such as the elaborate nautilus cup, that appear in some of his other compositions. Another version of the present work, signed and dated 1667, recently entered the collection of the Los Angeles County Museum of Art. In almost identical form the following motifs appear in both works: the silver dish with cantaloupe and peaches, the fruit still life composed of grapes and peaches, the *façon de Venise* glass, the architectural niche, and the draperies. Such a close relationship suggests that van Beyeren still had access to the San Francisco painting of 1666 when he composed the painting now in Los Angeles.

LFO

oil on canvas
139.8 x 116.5 cm
Signed with monogram and dated at upper left: *.AVBf./ .1666*
Gift of the de Young Museum Society
51.23.2

Provenance:
Possibly A. S. Drey, Munich; possibly von Lieblein collection, Vienna; Frederick Mont, New York; gift to the de Young, 1951.

Literature:
Scott A. Sullivan, 'A Banquet-Piece with Vanitas Implications', *The Bulletin of the Cleveland Museum of Art* 61 (October 1974), pp. 276–7, 282 n. 12, fig. 7; 'The Fine Arts Museums of San Francisco', *Apollo* 111, nos 216–17 (February–March 1980), pp. 210–11 n. 35.

Jan Steen
Dutch, 1626–1679

Much of Jan Steen's career took place in his native Leiden, where he enrolled at the university as a literature student in 1646 and joined the newly founded Guild of Saint Luke in 1648. The following year he married Margaretha, the daughter of the painter Jan van Goyen. After Margaretha's death, Steen married Maria van Egmont in 1673. Steen worked in The Hague from 1649 to 1654; lived in Delft for two years; spent the years from 1656 to 1660 in Warmond; 1661 to 1669 in Haarlem; and finally in 1670 settled again in his native Leiden, where he remained until his death. Contemporary sources are silent about his artistic training. However, his eighteenth-century biographers Arnold Houbraken and Jacob Campo Wyerman place him in the studio of Nicolas Knüpfer in Utrecht, in that of Adriaen van Ostade in Haarlem, and with Jan van Goyen in The Hague. Although some of these supposed influences are more difficult to discern in his work, the impact of Isaac van Ostade and of the Rembrandt pupil Jacob de West, both from The Hague, and of the Utrecht painter Joost Cornelisz. Droochsloot, can be demonstrated. Most of these artists are known primarily for their genre scenes and, with the exception of a small number of early landscapes, it was this subject matter that would occupy Steen throughout his career. However, in addition to a variety of genre types, including outdoor gatherings, tavern scenes, intimate interiors and riotous scenes of domestic upheaval, he painted serious biblical and mythological subjects. He developed into a versatile painter, able to work in both the broadly brushed style characteristic of the Haarlem school and the refined technique popularized by the Leiden *fijnschilder* (fine painters).

15
The Marriage of Tobias and Sarah.   c.1673

Steen is best known for his good-humoured depictions of Dutch society, works that are frequently characterized by a gentle mockery of the foibles of ordinary folk. To our delight, even his mythological and biblical paintings, such as this *Marriage of Tobias and Sarah*, are rendered in terms of everyday Dutch life. Set in an expansive seventeenth-century country house, the apocryphal story of Sarah and Tobias unfolds. The scene is rich in anecdotal detail and specific references to love and marriage borrowed from contemporary emblematic literature. While the elders review the terms of the contract, the young couple stands under a wreath of sunflowers, symbolic of constancy. The elegant Sarah, whose six previous husbands have been killed on their respective wedding nights by a demon, holds hands with the hopeful Tobias. He glances toward heaven with a gesture of entreaty for divine protection. Aid has indeed arrived, in the form of the archangel Raphael, who, situated between the bride and groom, will successfully drive out the demon, allowing Tobias to claim Sarah's dowry.

The artist has represented himself three times within the narrative. We recognize Steen at three different stages of life: as the youthful Tobias, as the seated notary, and as the man who stares out of the scene at us as he prepares to tap the wine cask. The fact that the artist has cast himself in several leading roles in the drama suggests that this composition commemorates his own second marriage in 1673 to Maria van Egmont. Typical of works from this period, the painting exhibits Steen's most accomplished technique, which renders in exquisite detail the surface textures of velvet cushion, oriental carpet, crockery, and the mauve satin of Sarah's wedding gown. *The Marriage of Tobias and Sarah* is a masterpiece of the artist's last decade.

LFO

oil on canvas
103.0 x 123.0 cm
Signed on base of table at lower right: *J. Steen*
Gift of the de Young Museum Society
62.12.1

Provenance:
Possibly anonymous sale, Amsterdam, auctioneer Jan Pietersz. Zoomer, 6 March 1708, no. 4; Mrs S. A. Westerhof, (née Henrietta van der Schagen), The Hague (her sale, Amsterdam, 16 May 1781, no. 53); traditionally Hoofman collection, The Hague and Haarlem; J. H. J. Quarles van Ufford, The Hague, before 1856; Charles J. Nieuwenhuys, London; Charles Auguste Louis Joseph, Duc de Morny, Paris (his sale,

Paris, 1 June 1865, no. 78); Prince Murat and descendants, Paris (sale, Paris, Palais Galeries, 2 March 1961, no. 157); Rosenberg & Stiebel, New York, and Frederick Mont, New York; purchased for the de Young, 1962.

Literature:
Tobias van Westrhene, *Jan Steen*, The Hague, 1856, no. 214bis; Baruch D. Kirschenbaum, *The Religious and Historical Paintings of Jan Steen*, New York and Montclair, New Jersey, 1977, pp. 63–4, 92–5, 121–3, fig. 86, pp. 217, 218, fig. 86a (detail).

Exhibited:
The Oakland Museum, *Art Treasures in California*, 1969, addendum.

Willem van Aelst
Dutch, 1627–1683

Willem van Aelst trained initially in his native Delft with his uncle, Evert van Aelst. Recorded as becoming a master of the Guild of Saint Luke at Delft on 9 November 1643, van Aelst travelled to France in 1645. In Paris he could have met Willem Kalf, the other leading Dutch still-life painter of the second half of the seventeenth century, whom he would re-encounter during his Amsterdam period. Van Aelst spent the years 1649 to 1656 working in Florence and Rome. As court painter to the Grand Duke of Tuscany, Ferdinand II de' Medici, he was in Florence at the same time as his compatriot Otto Marseus van Schriek. A certain stylistic indebtedness to this still-life painter has been noted in van Aelst's own compositions. Like other northern artists resident in Rome, he joined the Bentveughels (Birds of a Feather), a fraternity-like society, well known for its high-spirited antics. We deduce from the signature of a game piece dated 1658 (Amsterdam, Rijksmuseum) that van Aelst was known by the Bent nickname 'Scarecrow'. He returned to Delft in 1656 and by 1657 had settled permanently in Amsterdam. There he remained active until at least 1683, the year of his last dated painting, producing an abundance of fruit, flower and game pieces, as well as banquet still lifes. Rachel Ruysch is traditionally cited as the best known of van Aelst's students.

16
Flowers in a Silver Vase. 1663

Although signed in the Italian form of his name, the San Francisco *Flowers in a Silver Vase* dates from van Aelst's Amsterdam period. In a seemingly informal profusion of blooms and foliage, the artist carefully constructs a dynamic baroque composition. Dramatic lighting is employed, allowing the brilliantly coloured flowers to sparkle into full relief, as if protruding from the darkened background into our space. Equally baroque is the activation of the entire scene, beyond the objects' actual potential for movement. This is achieved by an insistence on the irregularity of the organic forms, which curve and countercurve out of and back into the mass of the bouquet. In addition, a pronounced diagonal is established across the pictorial surface, between the roses cascading from the silver vase, designed by the Amsterdam craftsman Johannes Lutma the Elder, and the red opium poppies reaching into the upper right corner of the canvas.

Despite the painting's compositional exuberance, van Aelst's technique is the tightly controlled style of the *fijnschilder* (fine painters). These artists, including the genre painters Gabriel Metsu, Gerard ter Borch and Frans van Mieris, achieve an exquisite finish through minutely rendered details, an approach particularly suited to the description of the surface textures of expensive material stuffs and richly variegated flowers.

The gaiety of the floral arrangement in *Flowers in a Silver Vase* is tempered by the inclusion of several traditional symbols of time's fleeting nature. Note particularly the open watch-case, whose tattered ribbon falls over the marble ledge, and the central tulip, which, well past its prime, has opened fully to drop its seeds. Such allusions to the transience of life and beauty invest this seemingly straightforward rendering of a bouquet of flowers with a moralizing aspect, transforming it into a *vanitas* still life, an essay on the vanity of life.

LFO

oil on canvas
67.5 x 54.5 cm
Signed and dated at lower left: *Guill.mo van aelst 1663*
Gift of Dr. and Mrs. Hermann Schuelein
51.21

Provenance:
Hawkins auction, London, 1936; Hermann Schuelein collection, New York, 1936?–51; gift to the de Young, 1951.

Exhibited:
The Hague, Mauritshuis; San Francisco, TFAMSF, *Great Dutch Paintings from America*, 1990–91, no. 1, colour repr.

Pieter de Hooch
Dutch, 1629–1684

Born in Rotterdam, the eldest son of a master bricklayer and a midwife, Pieter de Hooch was baptized on 20 December 1629 in the Reformed Church. Tradition has the young de Hooch working in the Haarlem studio of Nicolas Berchem along with Jacob Ochtervelt. However, following the baptismal record, no further mention of Pieter is found in contemporary documents until a citation in the city archives of Delft for August 1652. At that time he and the artist Hendrick van der Burgh witnessed a will, and both were listed as residents of Delft. De Hooch must have retained ties in Rotterdam, where he is recorded in 1654 at the time of his betrothal to Jannetze van der Burgh, Hendrick's sister. De Hooch had joined the Guild of Saint Luke in Delft by September 1655, and his early paintings include landscapes, guardroom scenes and stable interiors. The artist remained in Delft until moving permanently to Amsterdam by 1661, and the Delft years proved the most creative of his career. Paintings from this period exhibit a restrained harmony of composition and colour, which bespeaks the peaceful order of the domestic interiors de Hooch has re-created. This austerity of compositional means was compromised once he moved to the more cosmopolitan Amsterdam, where he catered to upper-middle-class patronage. Although his art was previously thought to have derived from that of his townsman Johannes Vermeer, it is now recognized that de Hooch was initially influenced by the domestic scenes of the Dordrecht artist Nicolaes Maes. Vermeer in turn drew on and refined the early innovations of both Maes and de Hooch. De Hooch died in a lunatic asylum in 1684, the year of his last dated painting.

17
Woman with Children in an Interior.   *c.*1658–60

The quiet realm of the middle-class home replaced the public religious and political institutions of seventeenth-century Dutch society as the focus of both life and art. In his most characteristic paintings, Pieter de Hooch celebrates the order and cleanliness of the bourgeois household, governed by the virtuous Dutch housewife. In this early painting from his Delft period, de Hooch is at his most lyrical, calling on compositional and colouristic harmonies to underscore the virtues of family life. What seems to be a simple transcription of the everyday is actually the result of the sophisticated manipulation of linear forms and modulation of colours to create a peaceful, light-filled environment for his figures.

The focus of *Woman with Children in an Interior* is the nurturing role of the mother as she tenderly gazes at the suckling child, while providing a model for her young daughter. This central theme is supported by the presence of several seemingly mundane objects that in fact carry a double meaning. This visual vocabulary of symbols would have been recognizable to seventeenth-century viewers who were familiar with contemporary emblematic literature. For example, the security of the bonds of marriage is suggested by the caged bird, the cupid featured in the relief decorating the hearth is a symbol of love, and the dog is a traditional symbol of fidelity and vigilance. The inclusion of these symbolic objects invests the genre scene with a rich moralizing texture, whereby contemporary mores are interpreted in terms of specific everyday occurrences.

A later variant of this composition, *Woman Peeling Apples* (London, Wallace Collection), features the same corner of a bourgeois Dutch interior.

LFO

oil on canvas
67.6 x 55.5 cm
Signed on footwarmer: *P. d Hooch*
Gift of the Samuel H. Kress Foundation
61.44.37

Provenance:
Possibly Pieter van Winter, Amsterdam, before 1807;
possibly Anna Louisa Agatha van Loon-van Winter,
Amsterdam, 1807–77; Gustave Baron de Rothschild,
Paris, 1877–c.1900; Robert Brakespeare, Henley-on-
Thames, Oxon., before 1916; M. Knoedler & Co., New
York, 1916; private collection, New York, 1925;
Katherine Mary Deere Butterworth, Moline, Illinois,
1925?–54 (her sale, New York, 1954); Frederick Mont,
New York, 1955; Samuel H. Kress Foundation, New
York, 1955–61; gift to the de Young, 1961.

Literature:
W. R. Valentiner, 'Pieter de Hooch: Part One', *Art in
America* 15 (December 1926), p. 61, fig. 6; 'Part Two',
15 (February 1927), p. 76, no. 15; Peter C. Sutton, *Peter
de Hooch*, Ithaca, NY, 1980, pp. 30, 83–4, no. 32, figs
30, 31, colour pl. VII; Simon Schama, *The
Embarrassment of Riches*, New York, 1987, pp. 540–2,
repr.

Exhibited:
New York, M. Knoedler & Co., *Loan Exhibition of
Dutch Masters of the Seventeenth Century*, 1925, no. 6,
repr.;
Washington, DC, National Gallery of Art, *Exhibition of
Art Treasures for America from the Samuel H. Kress
Collection*, 1961–62, no. 45;
Kansas City, Missouri, The Nelson Gallery of Art and
Atkins Museum, *Paintings of Seventeenth-Century
Dutch Interiors*, 1967–68, no. 6, repr. p. 11;
Philadelphia Museum of Art; Berlin, Gemäldegalerie;
London, Royal Academy of Arts, *Masters of
Seventeenth-Century Dutch Genre Painting*, 1984, no.
54, colour pl. 104;
The Hague, Mauritshuis; San Francisco, TFAMSF, *Great
Dutch Paintings from America*, 1990–91, no. 34,
colour repr.

Gerrit Adriaensz. Berckheyde
Dutch, 1638–1698

Baptized on 6 June 1638, Gerrit Berckheyde spent most of his active career in his native Haarlem. His earliest biographer, the eighteenth-century historian Arnold Houbraken, established the tradition that Gerrit was trained by his elder brother Job, himself a painter of cityscapes. Both brothers, however, owed much to the tradition of architectural painting popularized in Haarlem by Pieter Saenredam. Saenredam's work was accessible via original paintings and through an influential suite of prints after his views of Haarlem, etched by Jan van de Velde II. Before entering the Haarlem guild in July 1660, the Berckheyde brothers travelled in Germany, residing first in Cologne and then in Heidelberg. There they worked for Karl-Ludwig, Elector Palatinate. Upon returning to Holland the brothers again took up residence in Haarlem. Dated works by Gerrit survive from after the mid-1660s. In addition to a small number of landscapes and interiors, his painted oeuvre is composed of city views, principally featuring Haarlem, Amsterdam, The Hague and Cologne. At times Gerrit called on other artists, including Nicholas Guerrard, Johannes van Huchtenberg, Johannes Lingelbach and Dirck Maas, to paint the staffage figures in his townscapes. Most of the drawings identified as by Berckheyde are preparatory studies for paintings. He was buried in the Haarlem Janskerk on 14 June 1698, having drowned on the night of 10 June after spending the evening at a local tavern.

18
The Singel, Amsterdam.   1697

Signed and dated 1697, the San Francisco picture is one of several paintings by Berckheyde representing the Singel Canal, an easily identifiable landmark in Amsterdam. As with other favoured sites, the artist repeated this architectural scene, differentiating the present canvas from the other versions by variation in the figural elements. Here the staffage is particularly interesting as it seems to represent a specific historical event: the 1697 ceremonial progress of the Amsterdam burgomasters across the canal on the municipal barge, which, situated in the centre foreground, flies the city's coat of arms on the stern.

Berckheyde's viewpoint suggests that we, the viewers, are situated just before the open sluice, looking into the scene, much like the single figure on the right. From this vantage-point we can observe the activities taking place along the Singel, at a point known as the London Quay, where boats bound for England moored. The large domed structure on the left was built between 1668 and 1671 to designs by Adriaen Dorsman. The building, whose cupola was altered when rebuilt after a fire in 1822, was originally consecrated as the New Lutheran Church; still standing today, it is used as a convention centre. The restrained and classical forms of the dome contrast with the more Gothic quality of the distant Herring Packers' Tower (*Haringpakkerstoren*), which was destroyed by fire in 1829.

In this beautifully modulated essay in spatial recession, Berckheyde plots the movement of the ground plane into the distance in a slow, precisely calculated manner. The pronounced diagonals of the open sluice introduce us into the pictorial space. The gentle gradation of light–dark values in the shadows, coupled with the repetition of the vertical architectural elements, leads our attention into the depths of the scene. The pale coolness of the colour scheme underscores the cerebral nature of the composition; the underlying geometry of the pictorial arrangement is softened only by the painting's atmospheric quality and the Hobbema-like foliage interspersed with the architectural elements.

LFO

oil on canvas
70.5 x 91.0 cm
Signed and dated at lower left: *Gerrit Berkheÿde/1697*
Mildred Anna Williams Collection
1952.77

Provenance:
Martin B. Asscher, London; to Gebr. Douwes, Amsterdam; purchased by the CPLH, 1952.

Literature:
Karl M. Birkmeyer, 'Three Dutch Landscapes of the Seventeenth Century', *Bulletin CPLH* 12, nos 1–2 (May –June 1954), n.p., fig. 5.

Exhibited:
San Francisco, CPLH; The Toledo Museum of Art; Boston, Museum of Fine Arts, *Age of Rembrandt*, 1966–67, no. 63, repr.

British Paintings

Thomas Gainsborough
1727–1788

Thomas Gainsborough was born in Suffolk, the fifth son of a wool merchant. He studied at Saint Martin's Lane Academy in London from 1740 to 1748 with Hubert Gravelot, an engraver and illustrator in the French rococo style, and with Francis Hayman, a painter of small portrait groups. To support himself, Gainsborough copied and repaired seventeenth-century Dutch landscapes, notably those of Jan Wynants and Jacob van Ruisdael, which were popular with English collectors. He was an acknowledged landscape painter by 1748, when he presented *The Charterhouse* to the Foundling Hospital. He returned to Suffolk that year, eventually settling in Ipswich as a portrait painter. From 1759 to 1774 Gainsborough lived in Bath, the fashionable resort of the aristocracy, where he deliberately refined his portrait style in the manner of Anthony van Dyck. He exhibited at the Society of Artists in London from 1761 to 1768, when he was invited to be a founding member of the Royal Academy. After several disagreements with the Academy over the hanging of his pictures, he withdrew and exhibited his work annually from 1784 at Schomberg House, his London residence. Gainsborough died in August 1788, and later that year his great rival, Sir Joshua Reynolds, paid special tribute to this artist in his fourteenth discourse to the Royal Academy.

19
Samuel Kilderbee. c.1755

Samuel Kilderbee (1725–1813), an Ipswich attorney and longtime town clerk, was a lifelong friend of Thomas Gainsborough and acted as executor of his will. Kilderbee secured many commissions for the artist, and he and his family all sat for their portraits. Kilderbee accompanied Gainsborough on a sketching trip to the Lake District in 1783, and the two corresponded regularly. *Landscape with Country Carts* (see cat. no. 20) was a gift from the artist to his friend.

Gainsborough's direct, vigorous portrait of Kilderbee dates from his early Suffolk period when both men were in their mid-twenties. There is a mannered formality to the artist's early Ipswich portraits, which tend to be somewhat naïve and awkward in execution, although loyal likenesses of the sitters. In this ambitious three-quarter portrait, Gainsborough attempts the transition from his smaller paintings of full-length figures in a landscape setting to the more fluent, open, full-size portraits of his maturity. There are weaknesses of design here, notably in the lack of integration between the sitter and the sketchy landscape behind him, but the artist's solid modelling and sensitivity to his subject promise the fulfilment of his genius. The long brushstroke flattening the bridge of the nose and the crisp delineation of features are debts to Jean-Baptiste Vanloo, a French portraitist fashionable in England about 1740, while the motif of the dog looking up at his master may refer to a work by Titian (*Charles V with Hound*, Madrid, Museo del Prado). In spite of Gainsborough's reiterated dislike of 'face painting', his career as a portraitist demonstrates great range, sustained achievement and a sincere devotion to his sitters.

MCS

oil on canvas
125.0 x 100.0 cm
Gift of the M. H. de Young Endowment Fund
54479

Provenance:
Samuel Kilderbee, Ipswich; by family descent to Admiral Spencer de Horsey (his sale, London, Christie's, 14 June 1929, no. 47, as *Portrait of a Gentleman* by Gainsborough Dupont); bought by Daws; Arthur L. Nicolson, Surrey (his sale, New York, American Art Association, 18 May 1933, no. 34); bought by Julius H. Weitzner, Inc., New York; purchased for the de Young, 1933.

Literature:
Mary Woodall, *Thomas Gainsborough: His Life and Work*, London, 1949, pp. 38–9; Ellis Waterhouse, *Gainsborough*, London, 1958, p. 294, no. 407, pl. 44; John Hayes, *Gainsborough: Paintings and Drawings*, London, 1975, no. 30, fig. 57.

Exhibited:
London, The Tate Gallery, *Thomas Gainsborough*, 1980–81, no. 60, repr.;
Paris, Grand Palais, *Gainsborough*, 1981, no. 8, repr.

20
Landscape with Country Carts. c.1784–85

Gainsborough's fondness for landscape painting was evident from the beginning of his career. Susceptible to a variety of influences from Flanders, Holland and France, he was particularly interested in seventeenth-century Dutch landscape; this interest may have been nurtured not only by the similarity in appearance between East Anglia and Holland but also by the aggressive acquisition of Dutch pictures by English collectors. Gainsborough composed in his studio from assemblages of bits of wood, stones, vegetables and even dolls. His loose and atmospheric handling and his delicate sense of colour created a landscape style that is essentially artificial, closer to the artifice of the rococo than to nature.

This composition is based on a seventeenth-century Dutch landscape by Pieter de Molijn, an artist represented by three works in Gainsborough's personal art collection, which was sold in London in 1789. To de Molijn's model the artist has added a framing tree at the left, which not only encloses the rustic scene but adds a sense of vertical movement. While the scene recalls the lingering influence of the Dutch masters on Gainsborough's work, his treatment of the feathery foliage, gentle terrain, billowing clouds and soft light anticipate nineteenth-century romanticism. Gainsborough gave this landscape to his friend Samuel Kilderbee of Ipswich, whose portrait he had painted some thirty years earlier (see cat. no. 19).

MCS

oil on canvas
128.0 x 102.5 cm
Inscribed on label on reverse: *This Landskip, Painted by Mr. Gainsborough about the Year 1778, was given by him as his CHEF D'OEUVRE to Mr. Kilderbee of Ipswich in Memory of Friendship*
Roscoe and Margaret Oakes Collection
75.2.8

Provenance:
Samuel Kilderbee, Ipswich (his sale, London, Christie's, 30 May 1829, no. 125, as *Upright Landscape — Children Carrying Wood*); bought by Thomas Emmerson, Stratford Place, London; Brook Greville (his sale, London, Christie's, 30 April 1836, no. 79, as *Cottage in Woody Lane — Market Carts and Peasants*, Kilderbee Collection); bought by Norton; Sir Charles H. Coote, 10th Baronet, Ballyfin, Queen's County, Ireland,

before 1865; by family descent to Sir Ralph Algernon Coote, sold 1923; Countess de Kotzbue, New York (her sale, New York, Plaza Art Galleries, 28 January 1956, no. 352, as *The Hay Cart*); bought by John P. Nicolson, New York; Roscoe and Margaret Oakes, San Francisco, 1956; gift to TFAMSF, 1975.

Literature:
Ellis Waterhouse, *Gainsborough*, London, 1958, p. 294, no. 941a, pl. 202; John Hayes, *The Landscape Paintings of Thomas Gainsborough*, New York, 1982, vol. 1, pp. 164, 182, fig. 195, pp. 184 n. 18, 186 n. 73; vol. 2, no. 156, repr. p. 530.

Exhibited:
London, The Tate Gallery, *Thomas Gainsborough*, 1980–81, no. 149, repr.;
Paris, Grand Palais, *Gainsborough*, 1981, no. 72, repr.

Sir William Beechey
1753–1839

Born in Burford, Oxfordshire, William Beechey was trained for the law, moving from his first employer in Gloucestershire in the late 1760s to London. After meeting some students at the Royal Academy, he entered the Academy Schools in 1774, and exhibited at the Academy from 1776 to 1839, one of the longest careers in the history of the institution. After some instruction from Johann Zoffany, well known for his conversation pieces, Beechey moved to Norwich in 1782 and set up a successful practice with the financial assistance of his patron, Dr Strachey, a clergyman. In Norwich he began to paint life-size portraits. He returned to London in 1787, entering into a professional rivalry with John Hoppner and Sir Thomas Lawrence. In 1793 Beechey was named painter to Queen Charlotte, wife of George III; the Queen became a personal friend of the artist's family and acted as godmother to one of the Beechey children. The artist was elected a full member of the Royal Academy in 1798, the same year he was knighted. Beechey's ability to achieve a conscientious but aristocratic likeness, probing subtly into the characters of his sitters, made him a favourite portraitist in Georgian society.

21
Master James Hatch. 1796

Master James Hatch (1783–1804), the only son of James Hatch of Clayberry Hall, Essex, was a pupil at Eton College and later studied at Cambridge; he died in his twenty-first year after catching cold during a voyage from Scotland to the Hebrides. Hatch is shown here in 1796 in the military uniform he wore as Marshall's Attendant at the Montem, Eton's traditional procession to Salt Hill. The Montem, held every three years between 1561 and 1847, when the ceremony was abolished, consisted of a procession of fancifully dressed boys, who marched with banners flying and military bands playing, demanding alms on the way. Whereas the Senior King's scholar was always the Captain of the Montem, it was a singular honour to be named Marshall's Attendant, the leader of the procession.

The cult of *sensibilité* that flourished in the later eighteenth century, propelled in large part by the writings of the French philosopher Jean-Jacques Rousseau, created a vogue for appealing, sentimental portraits of children. Borrowing a formula from Lawrence, Beechey has silhouetted his young sitter against a low horizon and dramatic sky, with a view of Windsor Castle beyond the Thames on the left, and of Eton College on the right. The artist's palette of fresh, clear colour, largely unfaded with time, is admirably suited to the natural dignity of the youth. Beechey exhibited this picture at the Royal Academy in 1797 in a prestigious group of portraits that included four of the royal princesses, one of the Queen, and one of the Prince of Wales.

MCS

oil on canvas
185.4 x 133.4 cm
Signed and dated on rock at lower left: *W. Beechey, pint./1796*
Mildred Anna Williams Collection
1942.10

Provenance:
James Hatch, Esq., Clayberry Hall, Essex; by family descent to the Hon. William Keith Rous, Worstead House, Norfolk (his sale, London, Christie's, 29 June 1934, no. 51); Carroll Carstairs and Daniel H. Farr, New York; H. K. S. Williams, New York and San Francisco; gift to the CPLH, 1942.

Literature:
W. Roberts, *Sir William Beechey, R.A.*, London, 1907, p. 54; Gay Drake Davison, 'Portrait of Master James Hatch: Painting by Sir William Beechey', *Bulletin CPLH* 2, no. 11 (February 1945), pp. 82–4, cover repr.

Exhibited:
London, Royal Academy of Arts, 1797, no. 196; Houston, The Museum of Fine Arts, *George Washington's World*, 1954, no. 102, repr.

Sir Henry Raeburn
1756–1823

Born in Stockbridge, near Edinburgh, the second son of a mill owner, Henry Raeburn was orphaned at the age of six. In 1765 his brother placed him in George Heriot's hospital (a home for orphans), where he received a classical education and learned the rudiments of gentlemanly behaviour. From 1772 to 1778 he was apprenticed to James Gilliland, a goldsmith and jeweller, and began to paint miniatures. Largely self-taught as an artist, without formal classes in draughtsmanship or anatomy, Raeburn may have received some instruction from David Deuchar, an engraver and etcher. His first known attempt at full-scale portraiture is *George Chalmers*, c.1776 (Dunfermline, Town Council). In 1784, shortly before Raeburn left for Italy, he met Sir Joshua Reynolds, who gave him introductions to Pompeo Batoni and Gavin Hamilton. Although the Roman experience left little mark on his work, Raeburn was impressed by the sculpture he viewed and may have been inspired also to a fuller use of colour and chiaroscuro. He returned to Edinburgh at the age of thirty to become that city's leading portraitist. He visited London in 1819 to determine the feasibility of establishing a studio there, but the keen competition persuaded him to return to Edinburgh. There he worked in comparative isolation from the changing fashions in London, although he exhibited at the Royal Academy from 1792 to 1823. President of the Society of Scottish Painters in 1812, Raeburn was admitted to full membership of the Royal Academy in 1815, was knighted in 1822, and was appointed King's Limner and Painter for Scotland in 1823, the year he died.

22
Sir Duncan Campbell, Bart. *c.*1812

Duncan Campbell (1786–1842) was the eldest son of Alexander Campbell of Barcaldine and Glenure (Argyllshire), a member of the Scottish Faculty of Advocates. Here he wears the uniform of the Third Scots Fusilier Guards, with whom he served as captain during the Napoleonic Wars. He fought at Copenhagen, in the Walcheron Expedition, and at the Battle of Talavera in the Peninsular Campaign. He was created 1st Baronet of Barcaldine and Glenure in 1831, and died in Brussels.

Raeburn focused on the head as the mirror of character, and he is at his best when the features are pronounced and his modelling is deep and sculptural, as in this portrait. He has revealed the structure of the head by blocking in the forehead, chin and mouth directly onto the canvas with long brushstrokes. He made no drawings and had little knowledge of anatomy, but by copying (perhaps from a camera obscura) the shapes made by light and shadows, he learned to create images with strong presence. The candour of his likenesses is particularly striking.

Around 1812 Raeburn evolved a successful pattern of great simplicity that he used for a number of military portraits, posing the sitter three-quarter length against a plain, dark background from which the figure was detached by forceful lighting. *Sir Duncan Campbell* is a superb example of this formula, and here the dramatic effect is heightened by a vigorous, aristocratic stance, combined with a striking colour scheme of saturated red and gold.

MCS

oil on canvas
128.2 x 101.5 cm
Inscribed on reverse: *Sir Duncan Campbell. 1st Bart. of Barcaldine. Capt. Scots Fusiliers Guards. by Sir Henry Raeburn*
Roscoe and Margaret Oakes Collection
75.2.12

Provenance:
Sir Duncan Campbell, 1st Baronet of Barcaldine and Glenure; by family descent to Sir Duncan Alexander Dundas Campbell, 3rd Baronet, Ridgway Place, Wimbledon; Edward S. Moore, Lexington, Kentucky; Roscoe and Margaret Oakes, San Francisco, by 1955; gift to TFAMSF, 1975.

Literature:
James Grieg, *Sir Henry Raeburn, R.A.*, London, 1911, p. 40; David Irwin and Francina Irwin, *Scottish Painters at Home and Abroad, 1700–1900*, London, 1975, pp. 160, 430 n. 43, pl. 65; Duncan Macmillan, *Painting in Scotland: The Golden Age*, Oxford, 1986, p. 134.

Exhibited:
Indianapolis, Herron Museum of Art, *The Romantic Era: Birth and Flowering, 1750–1850*, 1965, no. 15, repr.;
The Oakland Museum, *Art Treasures in California*, 1969, repr.

John Constable
1776–1837

John Constable was born in East Bergholt, Suffolk, the son of a well-to-do mill owner. An early interest in drawing was encouraged by the connoisseur Sir George Beaumont and by the etcher and draughtsman J. T. ('Antiquity') Smith, and in 1799 Constable travelled to London and entered the Royal Academy Schools. He exhibited at the Royal Academy for the first time in 1802 and began making regular sketching and painting trips to rural parts of central and south-eastern England, developing his style of *plein-air* sketching. Larger, more finished compositions were worked up in the studio, and in 1819 Constable exhibited at the Academy the first of his six-foot canvases showing scenes from the Stour River valley. He was elected an associate of the Academy in 1819, but did not become a full member until 1829. The inclusion of three of his paintings in the Paris Salon of 1824 brought him to the excited attention of French artists, who saw in his work a new model of fidelity to nature. In later life, the vivid naturalism of his landscapes gave way to a looser, more expressionistic style. The lectures on landscape painting he presented in his last years, from 1833 to 1836, preserve a personal account of his theories and practices.

23
A View on Hampstead Heath with Harrow in the Distance. 1822

This beautifully fresh and fluid oil sketch on paper is representative of a long series of paintings Constable made out of doors on Hampstead Heath in the early 1820s. The Constables, who had a residence in London, first took a house in Hampstead for the late summer of 1819. Thereafter, they rented a house at Hampstead every year (except 1824) until 1827, when they settled into a more permanent home there. Constable's earliest known painting of a Hampstead subject dates from October 1819 (London, Victoria and Albert Museum). He worked regularly on the heath during his sojourns in Hampstead, painting a variety of motifs, including many cloud studies, directly from nature, as he intently followed the changing effects on the landscape of weather, atmosphere, light and seasons. The oil sketch afforded a perfect medium for the rapid notation of his direct observations.

Many of Constable's sketches look westward across the heath toward the village of Harrow in the distance. Here, the spire of the church in Harrow is glimpsed in the extreme distance along the horizon just to the left of centre. A path, with two figures on it, leads diagonally to the top of the plain in the middle ground. Several figures are seen under the trees at the left, and a man and his horse stand as a strong accent along the right margin. The main subject of the painting, however, is the rosy light from the setting sun that fills the sky and warms the landscape in the foreground. A label on the back of the painting inscribed *Sunday Augst. 25, 1822 After Sunset* shows Constable's concern for fixing the exact circumstances of his sketches: the label is not written in the artist's hand but almost certainly reproduces an original inscription no longer visible.

The mistaken identification of this scene, as showing the Gospel Oak, near Jack Straw's Castle, derives from an exhibition of the work at the South Kensington Museum in 1880 with an incorrect title (recorded on a second label on the reverse).

SAN

oil on paper mounted on canvas
30.8 x 50.2 cm
Inscribed on labels on reverse: *Hampstead Heath. Sunday Augst. 25, 1822 After Sunset.* and *GOSPEL OAK, Near Jack Straw's Castle, Hampstead, 1822. b. 1776. J. Constable R.A. d.1837. Lent by Mrs. Constable.*
Bequest of Whitney Warren, Jr., in memory of Mrs. Adolph B. Spreckels
1988.10.40

Provenance:
Charles Golding Constable, the artist's son; Captain and Mrs A. M. Constable (their sale, London, Christie's, 11 July 1887, no. 76); to Hughes; Dr H. A. C. Gregory, 1949; Thomas Agnew & Sons, London; A. L. Dewar,

1956; Whitney Warren, Jr., San Francisco; bequeathed to TFAMSF, 1988.

Literature:
Robert Hoozee, *L'opera completa di Constable*, Milan, 1979, no. 339, repr.; Graham Reynolds, *The Later Paintings and Drawings of John Constable*, New Haven and London, 1984, vol. 1, no. 22.19; vol. 2, pl. 346.

Exhibited:
London, South Kensington Museum, 1880, no. 12; London, Arts Council of Great Britain, *An Exhibition of Sketches and Drawings by John Constable from the Collection of Dr H. A. C. Gregory*, 1949, no. 15; Manchester City Art Gallery, *John Constable, 1776–1837*, 1956, no. 37.

John Martin
1789–1854

John Martin was largely a self-taught artist, who achieved through his vivid imagination and bold, theatrical style an epitome of the romantic sublime in landscape painting, and whose work proved highly influential. Born in East Landends near Haydon Bridge on the Tyne River, he moved with his family to Newcastle in 1803 and there received some slight training from the Italian painter Boniface Musso. In 1806 Martin went to London and during the next five or six years supported himself as a painter on porcelain and glass. His earliest exhibits at the Royal Academy and British Institution in 1812–14, however, marked the emergence of an original talent, and he quickly gained fame for his vast, densely detailed scenes of tumult and disaster. So audacious were some of his visions that he received the nickname 'Mad Martin'. A lifelong foe of the Royal Academy, he was one of its most bitter critics in parliamentary hearings on the Academy in 1836. In the 1820s, Martin turned his attention to engravings and mezzotints, partly as a way of reaching a larger audience, and his illustrations of Milton's *Paradise Lost* and of the Bible proved particularly popular. He also worked as an inventor and pamphleteer and proposed a number of ideas for public works. In France, his name became synonymous with the sublime, and his work formed a direct link to the American landscape tradition of Thomas Cole, Washington Allston and Frederic Church.

24
The Assuaging of the Waters. 1840

As a primary contributor to romanticism's iconography of catastrophe and cataclysm, Martin turned inevitably to the biblical story of the Deluge for one of his themes, continuing the vogue for this subject established by such artists as Philip James de Loutherbourg, J. M. W. Turner and Anne-Louis Girodet-Trioson. He exhibited a first version of *The Deluge* at the British Institution in 1826 and explained in an accompanying pamphlet his intentions of careful historical reconstruction. This work is now lost, but in 1834 Martin painted a larger and even more tumultuously dramatic version (New Haven, Connecticut, Yale Center for British Art), which he exhibited with great success at the Paris Salon of 1835. In 1833 he had made a mezzotint illustrating the eve of the Deluge, and in 1838 he exhibited the watercolour *The Assuaging of the Waters* (now lost), showing the aftermath of the flood, evidence that he may have been considering a full cycle of paintings on the subject. Martin's opportunity for such a series came in 1839 when Prince Albert, who visited the artist's studio to survey progress on his painting *The Coronation of Queen Victoria* (London, The Tate College), commissioned from him a large *Eve of the Deluge* (London, The Royal Collection). The Prince may also have been instrumental in persuading the Duchess of Sutherland, Mistress of the Robes to Queen Victoria, to commission *The Assuaging of the Waters* as a sequel. Martin exhibited the last two works from his trilogy at the Royal Academy in 1840 and published another pamphlet to explain his narrative program.

In the pamphlet, he wrote about *The Assuaging of the Waters*:

In this picture I have chosen the period after the Deluge, when I suppose the sun to have burst forth over the broad expanse of waters gently rippled by the breeze, which is blowing the storm clouds seaward; in the distance just beyond the horizontal line is the Ark in the full flood of sunlight. The direction of land is indicated by the tops of mountains which are beginning to appear; that in the foreground shining in the bright beams of the sun; nearer still is a rock covered with sea weeds, coral and shells; and in a still pool left by the subsiding waters are the lotus flower and the Nautilus.

Martin has included a drowned serpent and a black raven as symbolic of original sin and old-world corruption. A white dove plucks an olive branch, which it will take back to Noah as evidence of new lands. In accordance with the theme of hope and rebirth, Martin's colour in this painting is unusually bright and clear. The sun breaking through the parting clouds casts an iridescent light on the whole scene. The artist's handling of paint is also unusually varied, from the porcelain-like finish of the distant horizon, to the foamy, transparent crests of the waves, to the loose and almost abstract textures of the foreground rocks. Produced when Martin was fifty-one, this work is one of his key images and shows him still experimenting with technique.

SAN

oil on canvas
143.5 x 218.0 cm
Signed and dated at lower right: *J. Martin 1840*
Museum purchase, Whitney Warren, Jr., Fund, in
memory of Mrs. Adolph B. Spreckels
1989.73

Provenance:
Commissioned by Lady Harriet Howard, Duchess of
Sutherland, Stafford House, London; the General
Assembly of the Church of Scotland, by 1953 (sale,
London, Sotheby's, 9 March 1988, no. 90); to Richard L.
Feigen & Co., New York; purchased by TFAMSF, 1989.

Literature:
Thomas Balston, *John Martin, 1789–1854: His Life
and Works*, London, 1947, pp. 203–4; Christopher

Johnstone, *John Martin*, London and New York, 1974,
pp. 23, 74–5, repr. pp. 76–7; William Feaver, *The Art
of John Martin*, Oxford, 1975, pp. 161–4, 231 n. 20,
232 n. 38, pl. 122, colour pl. VIb; Steven A. Nash,
'John Martin's *Assuaging of the Waters*', *Triptych* [San
Francisco], no. 50 (April–May 1990), pp. 10–11, colour
repr.

Exhibited:
London, Royal Academy of Arts, 1840, no. 509;
London, Whitechapel Art Gallery, *John Martin*, 1953,
no. 29;
Sheffield, Mappin Art Gallery, *Victorian Paintings*,
1968, no. 3;
Newcastle, Laing Art Gallery, *John Martin, 1789–1854:
Artist, Reformer, Engineer*, 1970, no. 24, pl. 6.

Seventeenth- and Eighteenth-Century French Paintings

Georges de La Tour
1593–1652

The son of a baker in the independent province of Lorraine, Georges de La Tour is first mentioned in documents in 1616, when he was still living in Vic. By 1620 he had established himself in Lunéville and had hired his first apprentice. He made a visit to Paris in 1639, the same year he was named *peintre ordinaire du roi* to Louis XIII. While little is known about La Tour's life or artistic training, he may have been in Rome from 1610 to 1616 and may also have gone to the Netherlands. Although La Tour was famous in his lifetime, his reputation fell into oblivion after his death; his work was rediscovered only in the twentieth century. Scholarly opinion remains divided over the chronology of his oeuvre, but La Tour's important position as a dramatist of humble reality is universally acknowledged today.

25
Old Man.   c.1618–19

oil on canvas
91.0 x 60.5 cm
Roscoe and Margaret Oakes Collection
75.2.9

Provenance:
E. Holzscheiter, Meilen, Switzerland, c.1930; Vitale Bloch, 1954; Galerie des Tourettes, Paris, by 1955; M. Knoedler & Co., New York, 1955; to Roscoe and Margaret Oakes, San Francisco, 1956; gift to TFAMSF, 1975.

Literature:
Jacques Thuillier, *Tout l'oeuvre peint de Georges de La Tour*, Paris, 1973, nos 2–3, reprs, colour pl. 1–2;

Thierry Bajou, *De La Tour*, Paris, 1985, pp. 11, 22, colour reprs, pp. 34, 36, 113; *French Paintings*, pp. 61–4, colour reprs.

Exhibited:
Rome, Palazzo delle Esposizioni, *Il seicento europeo: Realismo, classicismo, barocco*, 1956–57, nos 158–9; Cleveland Museum of Art, *Caravaggio and His Followers*, 1971–72, nos 40–1, reprs; Paris, Musée de l'Orangerie, *Georges de La Tour*, 1972, nos 1–2, reprs; Paris, Grand Palais; New York, The Metropolitan Museum of Art; The Art Institute of Chicago, *France in the Golden Age: Seventeenth-Century French Painting in American Collections*, 1982, nos 35–6, reprs.

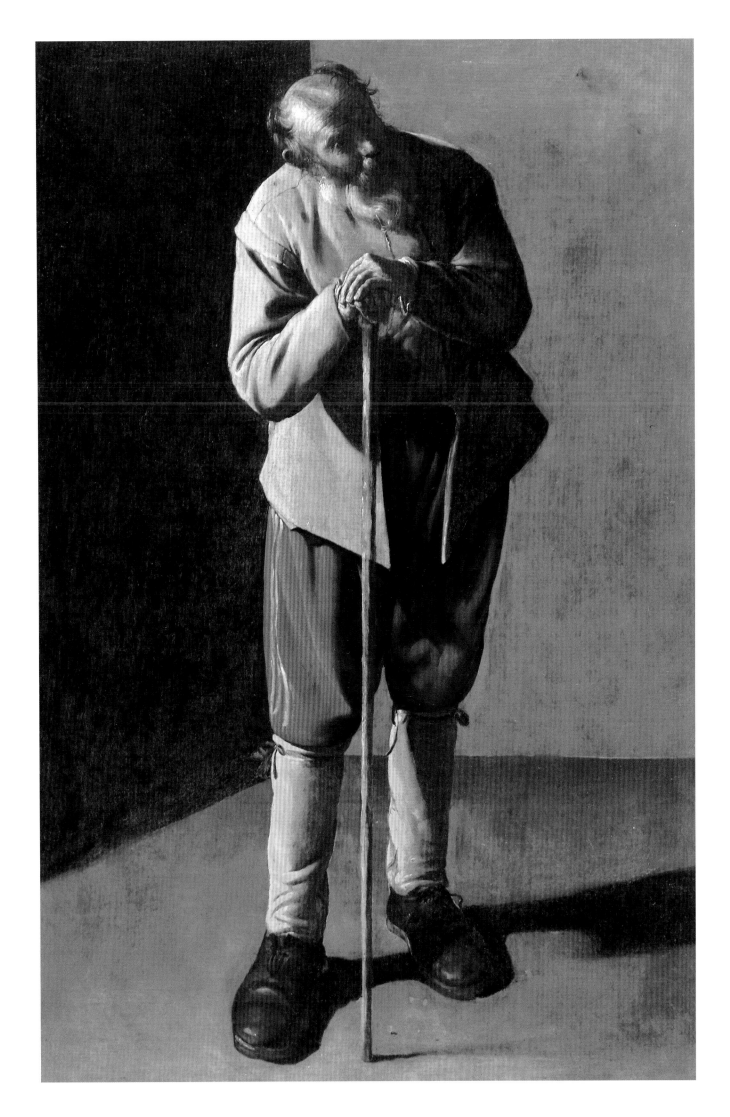

26
Old Woman. c.1618–19

Although the attribution of these paintings has been challenged in the past, they are now accepted as outstanding examples of La Tour's early period (before he settled in Lunéville), when he executed powerful vernacular images of destitute musicians, tattered beggars, and old men. Paintings closely related in artistic, thematic and chronological terms to San Francisco's paintings are the *Hurdy Gurdy Player, c.1618–19* (Bergues, Musée Municipal), *Old Peasant Couple Eating, c.1620* (Berlin, Gemälde-galerie), and *Beggars' Brawl, c.1625–30* (Malibu, California, J. Paul Getty Museum).

Old Man and *Old Woman* have been described at times as depicting peasants, perhaps from Italy or Lorraine. However, the costumes, particularly the woman's embroidered apron, suggest that these are not simple peasants, but perhaps figures from the popular theatre of northern Europe — Alison, the irascible, domineering wife, and Père Dindon, the docile, henpecked husband. Although the characters may be engaged in a bitter verbal exchange, La Tour presents them without sentiment or elaboration.

The strong lighting emphasizing the shadows may emanate from footlights, but this chiaroscuro technique also reflects the influence of the Italian artist Caravaggio or the Utrecht masters who imitated him. La Tour's skilful execution and subtle use of colour combine here to create two of his most ingenious works.

MCS

oil on canvas
91.5 x 60.5 cm
Roscoe and Margaret Oakes Collection
75.2.10

Provenance:
Same as for *Old Man.*

Literature:
Same as for *Old Man.*

Exhibited:
Same as for *Old Man.*

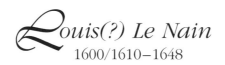

Louis(?) Le Nain
1600/1610–1648

In spite of intensive study, the oeuvre of the three Le Nain brothers — Louis, Antoine and Mathieu — remains difficult to attribute with complete assurance. Born in Laon in northern France to a family of property but of peasant origins, the brothers all elected an artistic career, moving to Paris by 1629. There they worked together in the same studio, collaborated on some works, and signed their paintings simply *Le Nain*. They produced not only genre paintings but portraits, mythologies and religious pictures as well. They were patronized by the aristocracy and their paintings were prized by connoisseurs. The brothers participated in the first session of the Royal Academy of Painting and Sculpture in 1648. Both Antoine and Louis died that same year, presumably victims of a contagious disease. Mathieu is the youngest and best documented of the brothers, but information on Antoine and Louis is often too vague for firm distinctions to be made between the two. However, Louis has been traditionally assigned the peasant scenes that depict people with round, heavy faces and a melancholy air (*The Cart*, 1641, and *Peasant Meal*, 1642, both Paris, Musée du Louvre). His technique is more fluent, his work has more breadth, and his sombre colour schemes reflect a serious, thoughtful temperament. The Le Nains refused to embrace the prevailing tenets of French classicism, adhering instead to the realist tradition by portraying ordinary people from their provincial boyhood. They were painters of reality, and their work remains fundamental to the artistic heritage of France.

27
Peasants before Their House. c.1641

The realistic strain in seventeenth-century French art is typically northern European, yet it derives from the influence of Caravaggio, who worked in Rome. Peasant life as depicted by the Dutch and Flemish contemporaries of the Le Nains tends to be vivacious, temporal and often anecdotal. The rustic scenes associated with Louis Le Nain are completely original in their gravity of conception and tranquil dignity. The artist's peasants are specifically French, but there is a classical quality in their statuesque grouping and the immobility of their poses, as well as a spirituality in the silent expectancy of their expressions.

In this painting the artist has used a monochromatic palette of greys and ochres to describe the peasants' clothing, the earth and the sky. Subdued tones of yellow bring out the weathered old stones of the Laon farmhouse. Only two bold touches of red relieve the sombre canvas. Diffused light from an overcast sky bathes the austerity and misery of the surroundings. Against this background stands the rugged figure of a man in a hat, whom Jacques Thuillier has described in the 1978–79 exhibition catalogue as being 'in his tattered clothes, one of the most beautiful figures of a peasant in all of French art'. There is neither sentiment nor humour in this scene, but rather a sincerity of observation in which the human element is paramount. Another version of this composition, considered a copy, is in the Museum of Fine Arts, Boston.

MCS

oil on canvas
55.0 x 70.5 cm
Mildred Anna Williams Collection
1941.17

Provenance:
Dukes of Rutland, Belvoir Castle, England, last third of eighteenth century–1929; M. Knoedler & Co., New York, 1936; purchased by the CPLH, 1941.

Literature:
Paul Jamot, *Les Le Nain*, Paris, 1929, pp. 40, 43, 48, repr. p. 57; Vitale Bloch, 'Louis Le Nain and His Brothers', *Burlington Magazine* 75, no. 437 (1939), p. 53; *French Paintings*, pp. 65–8, colour repr.

Exhibited:
Reims, Musée des Beaux-Arts, *Les Le Nain*, 1953, no. 7, pl. 5;
Paris, Grand Palais, *Les Frères Le Nain*, 1978–79, no. 35, repr., colour reprs pp. 10, 205 (details);
Paris, Grand Palais; New York, The Metropolitan Museum of Art; The Art Institute of Chicago, *France in the Golden Age: Seventeenth-Century French Painting in American Collections*, 1982, no. 46, repr.

Eustache Le Sueur
1616–1655

The eighteenth century ranked Eustache Le Sueur with Nicolas Poussin and Raphael, but posterity has not esteemed him as highly. Many of his great decorative ensembles, such as the Cabinet de l'Amour and the Chambre des Muses for the Hôtel Lambert, have been dispersed (Paris, Musée du Louvre), a number of canvases have disappeared, and some of his most famous works survive in poor condition. The son of an illiterate artisan, Le Sueur was born and lived his entire life in Paris. Apprenticed as a boy to Simon Vouet, the most influential French artist of the era, he was exposed to the art of antiquity and Italian painting by visits to Parisian collections and the Château de Fontainebleau, and he refined his taste by contacts with the cultural leaders of seventeenth-century Paris. Vouet assisted his favourite pupil with commissions at the beginning of his career, but Le Sueur's reputation was firmly established with his *Life of Saint Bruno*, 1645–48 (Paris, Musée du Louvre), a series of twenty-two pictures executed for the cloister of the Charterhouse of Paris. As a history painter, the artist became a founding member of the Royal Academy of Painting and Sculpture in 1648, receiving commissions from royalty, the church, and private patrons. The death of this 'French Raphael' at the age of thirty-eight, followed closely by many of the leading painters of his generation, cleared the way for Charles Le Brun's ascendancy to the role of artistic dictator of France during the reign of Louis XIV.

28
Sleeping Venus.   *c.*1640

Le Sueur combines the talents of a great decorative painter with the spirituality of a religious painter. Although his early work has been confused with that of his master, Vouet, Le Sueur's style can be distinguished by a richness of inspiration, a note of sensuality, and a refined use of colour. Around 1640 his art gradually became more linear in style and classical in subject matter, without losing its characteristic elegance, harmony and luminosity of tone.

The mythological tale of Vulcan, god of fire, and Venus, goddess of love, is used here by Le Sueur as a pretext for his primary artistic interest: the female nude. Using a highly decorative colour scheme of warm red, rich blue and cold white, the artist creates a sense of drama by emphasizing the languorous, erotic form of the sleeping goddess in contrast to the more muted figures of Cupid and Vulcan, seen at his forge in the background. The pose of Venus is indebted to an ancient sculpture, *Sleeping Ariadne* (Vatican, Pio-Clementine Museum); this pose was later repeated in Titian's painting *The Andrians*, 1523–25 (Madrid, Museo del Prado), as well as in Jean-Auguste-Dominique Ingres's various *odalisques*. Le Sueur's celebrated composition was copied several times and was engraved by Pierre Daret and Pierre-François Basan.

MCS

oil on canvas
122.0 x 117.0 cm (octagonal)
Mildred Anna Williams Collection
1977.10

Provenance:
Probably Prince de Conti, Paris (his sale, Paris, 8 April 1777, no. 621); bought by Vautrin; O'Dwyer, Salisbury, England, *c.*1940–68; Johannes Thermes, Dublin, 1969–75; Art Associates Partnership, Bermuda, 1975; purchased by TFAMSF, 1977.

Literature:
Alain Mérot, *Eustache Le Sueur, 1616–1655*, Neuilly-sur-Seine, 1987, no. 14, fig. 12, colour pl. LV; *French Paintings*, pp. 69–73, colour repr.

Exhibited:
Paris, Grand Palais; New York, The Metropolitan Museum of Art; The Art Institute of Chicago, *France in the Golden Age: Seventeenth-Century French Painting in American Collections*, 1982, no. 51, colour repr.

Nicolas de Largillierre
1656–1746

Although born in Paris, Nicolas de Largillierre spent his youth in Antwerp, becoming a student of the still-life and genre painter Antoine Goubau in 1668. Soon after his acceptance as a master in the Guild of Saint Luke (1672), Largillierre went to England. There he studied portraiture, perhaps in the studio of Peter Lely. He returned to Paris in 1679 and became a member of the Royal Academy of Painting and Sculpture in 1686, advancing rapidly to important posts in the hierarchy of that institution. The major part of his work was devoted to portraiture, but Largillierre also produced history paintings, landscapes and still lifes. His rival for court commissions was Hyacinthe Rigaud, while his own clientele was primarily the wealthy bourgeoisie, who found his taste for warm colour tones, sumptuous fabrics and a regal manner of presentation very much to their liking. Extremely successful during his long life, the artist produced a huge oeuvre. Anthony van Dyck's influence on English portraiture, as well as the seventeenth-century French portrait tradition, were critical to his stylistic development. Largillierre is pivotal in the transition from the baroque to the rococo portrait style during the reigns of Louis XIV and Louis XV.

29
Portrait of a Gentleman. 1710

The identity of this sitter remains unknown. By 1928 he was said to be the Marquis de Montespan, husband of one of Louis XIV's most famous mistresses. However, the Marquis died in 1702, eight years before this portrait was painted, and no likeness of him that might be used for comparative purposes has been discovered. In 1981 the gentleman was identified as Victor-Marie, Marquis de Coeuvres, Duc d'Estrées, a *maréchal* of France, because of his strong resemblance to the subject of an engraving by Jean Audran after a lost portrait by Largillierre. However, a replica of that portrait survives at Versailles, depicting a man with blue eyes, rather than the brown eyes of this sitter. Also, it is unlikely that a recipient of the Order of Saint Esprit, which the *maréchal* received in 1705, would choose to be portrayed without it.

Neither the pose nor the costume of the sitter is unique in Largillierre's work. Another portrait, strikingly similar except for the face and minor details, and also signed and dated 1710, was identified in 1928 as that of a Parisian tax collector, *La Live de Belle-garde* (Paris, private collection). It may seem surprising that the artist repeated himself in two portraits executed in the same year, but the level of production in Largillierre's studio was so intense that poses, clothing and accessories were frequently reused.

Although this painting repeats a formula, the sitter's face has not been idealized, and his distinct personality is revealed. His rich, elegant costume suggests affluence and social position. Dramatic in impact, this portrait exemplifies the grand manner that characterized portraiture during the reign of Louis XIV. However, there is evidence of a freer, less ostentatious style evolving in the artist's fluid, unlaboured execution and warm, vibrant colour scheme.

MCS

oil on canvas
135.5 x 105.0 cm
Signed and dated at lower left: *Peint par N./De Largillierre. 1710*
Gift of Archer M. Huntington through Herbert Fleishhacker
1929.1

Provenance:
Perhaps Prince Sigismond Radziwill; probably sale, Paris, Hôtel Drouot, 15 April 1868, no. 36; probably M. Marquiset (estate sale, Paris, Hôtel Drouot, 28–29 April 1890, no. 22); Comte André de Ganay, after 1890; Comte Jean de La Riboisière, Paris; Lord Edgar V. d'Abernon, London, c.1928; Duveen Bros., Paris (on

consignment from Lord d'Abernon); purchased by the CPLH, 1929 (as *Marquis de Montespan*).

Literature:
Georges de Lastic, 'Largillierre à Montréal', *Gazette des beaux-arts* 102 (July–August 1983), p. 78; *French Paintings*, pp. 210–12, colour repr.

Exhibited:
Paris, Petit Palais, *Exposition N. de Largillierre*, 1928, no. 29 (1st ed.), no. 32 (2nd ed.) (as *Marquis de Montespan*);
Montreal Museum of Fine Arts, *Largillierre and the Eighteenth-Century Portrait*, 1981, no. 23, repr. (as *Duc d'Estrées*).

Jean-Antoine Watteau
1684–1721

Considered the greatest painter of early-eighteenth-century France, Jean-Antoine Watteau was born in Valenciennes, then part of Flanders. He went to Paris around 1702 and became acquainted with Pierre Mariette, who enabled him to study the works of such artists as Jacques Callot, Titian and Peter Paul Rubens. In the studio of Claude Gillot, Watteau learned theatrical themes, and through Claude Audran, concierge of the Luxembourg Palace, he had the revelatory experience of studying Rubens's Marie de Médicis cycle (now Paris, Musée du Louvre). Watteau returned to Valenciennes in 1710 and there produced scenes of military life. Upon arriving again in Paris, he met Pierre Crozat, a wealthy amateur, whose collection of drawings was to prove influential in the perfection of the artist's craft. In 1717 Watteau was elected to membership in the Royal Academy of Painting and Sculpture with his *Pilgrimage to the Island of Cythera* (Paris, Musée du Louvre); he was elected to the Academy as a painter of *fêtes galantes*, a genre created especially for him, and one that he refined and amplified as his own pictorial invention. He travelled to England in 1719–20, but poor health brought him back to France, where he died at the age of thirty-seven. Watteau's personal style, characterized by a delicate palette and sensitivity to atmosphere, brought him great acclaim during his lifetime.

30
The Foursome [La Partie quarrée].   c.1713

Although this celebrated painting is neither signed nor dated, tradition associates it with three other paintings of similar theme executed by Watteau around 1712–13. All were included in the *Recueil Jullienne* (1739), a collection of engravings after Watteau's drawings and paintings. Jean Moyreau published an engraving after *La Partie quarrée* in 1731, François Boucher engraved the figure of Gilles/Pierrot, and Jean-Auguste-Dominique Ingres made a drawing after the composition.

Watteau made a number of preparatory drawings for *The Foursome*, and X-rays indicate that he hesitated before deciding on the position of the heroine's head. This lady appears again in a similar pose in *The Pleasures of the Ball* (London, The Dulwich Picture Gallery).

In his *fêtes galantes*, the artist's delicate figures, shimmering fabrics and soft, atmospheric effects evoke an Arcadian dreamland of music, conversation and amorous dalliance. Although the term can be defined simply as a party with two couples, the licentious implication of *La Partie quarrée* remains unchanged from the eighteenth century. As the last rays of the sun give their costumes a brilliant sheen, four characters from the *commedia dell'arte* (Pierrot, Mezzetin and their ladies) converse in a park, but the exact meaning of the scene is unknown. The union of observation and fantasy plus ambiguity of intent and erotic connotations is characteristic of Watteau's best work.

MCS

oil on canvas
49.5 x 63.0 cm
Mildred Anna Williams Collection
1977.8

Provenance:
Possibly Dr Robert Bragge (his sale, London, 17 March 1758, no. 77); acquired by Robert Harenc (or Harene); probably Bondon sale, Paris, 30 May–1 June 1839, no. 114; perhaps Baron Llangattock, England, c.1907; 2nd Baron Llangattock, England (his sale, London, Christie's, 28 November 1958, no. 79); acquired by Galerie Cailleux, Paris; purchased by TFAMSF, 1977.

Literature:
Ettore Camesasca and Pierre Rosenberg, *Tout l'oeuvre*

peint de Watteau, Paris, 1970, no. 82, repr.; Marianne Roland Michel, *Watteau: An Artist of the Eighteenth Century*, London, 1984, pp. 35, 69, 115, 177, 211, 212, 215, 307, fig. 175, pl. 10, colour details; Donald Posner, *Antoine Watteau*, Ithaca, NY, 1984, pp. 9, 10, 20, 57, 69, 243, colour repr.; *French Paintings*, pp. 324–8, colour repr.

Exhibited:
Paris, Galerie Cailleux, *Watteau et sa génération*, 1968, no. 35, repr.;
Washington, DC, National Gallery of Art; Paris, Grand Palais; Berlin, Schloss Charlottenburg, *Watteau, 1684–1721*, 1984–85, no. 14, colour repr.

Jean-Marc Nattier
1685–1766

Jean-Marc Nattier succeeded Hyacinthe Rigaud as the leading court portraitist of France. The son and brother of artists, he began his studies under the sponsorship of his godfather, Jean-Baptiste Jouvenet. Nattier received early professional encouragement from Louis XIV when, in 1701, he presented his drawing for the engraving after Rigaud's full-length portrait of the King. He was also influenced by Charles Le Brun and Peter Paul Rubens, whose paintings he copied in Paris. In 1717 he went to Holland to work for Peter the Great and the next year was elected to membership in the Royal Academy of Painting and Sculpture. Thereafter he specialized in oil and pastel portraits, depicting the sitters as mythological figures. While reminiscent of a genre popular in the sixteenth century, these works are completely different in spirit. Nattier portrayed many of the leading members of the court of Louis XV, but his reputation is firmly based on his portraits of the King, Queen Marie Leszczyńska and their daughters. He excelled as a painter of women, flattering his sitters by endowing them with the attributes of goddesses of Olympus and posing them against a backdrop of classical columns, sumptuous draperies, and decorative elements.

31
Thalia, Muse of Comedy. 1739

oil on canvas
136.0 x 124.5 cm
Signed and dated at lower left: *Nattier pinxit 1739*
Mildred Anna Williams Collection
1954.59

Provenance:
Baron Albert de Rothschild, Vienna; to Baron Louis de Rothschild, Vienna; Rosenberg & Stiebel, New York; purchased by the CPLH, 1954.

Literature:
French Paintings, pp. 226–9, colour repr.

Exhibited:
Houston, The Museum of Fine Arts, *A Magic Mirror: The Portrait in France, 1700–1900*, 1986–87, no. 7, repr. p. 20, colour repr. p. 127 (detail).

32
Terpsichore, Muse of Music and Dance. *c.*1739

These paintings, presumed pendants, were acquired by the museum as portraits of the Nesle sisters — the Duchesse de Châteauroux and the Marquise de Vintimille — both mistresses of Louis XV, in the guises of Thalia, Muse of Comedy, and Euterpe, Muse of Music. These identifications are easily disproved by comparing the San Francisco paintings with documented likenesses of the proposed sitters, and the revealing costumes of the mythological personifications appear inappropriate for these noble ladies. In addition, the previously curved outline of the canvases, visible in the upper corners, lends credence to the belief that the pictures were conceived as decorative overdoors. Both compositions have been copied.

The subjects are in fact Thalia, Muse of Comedy, with her ivy crown and dark mask, and Terpsichore, Muse of Music and Dance, with her lyre and plectrum. Thalia raises a velvet curtain on a theatrical scene, while Terpsichore poses before a group of dancers and musicians. The youth and vivacity of these charming nymphs are presented with Nattier's characteristic ease and intimacy, luminous colour — particularly the rich blue of Thalia's drapery — and sweetness of facial expression, enhanced by the artifice of rouge.

In choosing a model for Thalia, it is probable that Nattier turned to Silvia Balletti, a popular actress of the Comédie Italienne in Paris, who created many roles in the plays of Marivaux. She was the subject of a number of portraits by various artists including Nattier, who portrayed her about 1745, also wearing an ivy crown (location unknown).

MCS

oil on canvas
136.0 x 125.0 cm
Mildred Anna Williams Collection
1954.60

Provenance:
Same as for *Thalia, Muse of Comedy.*

Literature:
French Paintings, pp. 230–2, colour repr.

Nicolas Lancret
1690–1743

Nicolas Lancret came from a family of Parisian artisans. After an apprenticeship with the history painter Pierre Dulin, and a term at the Royal Academy's school, he entered Claude Gillot's studio in 1712. Gillot, then director of scene designs and costumes for the Opéra, probably introduced Lancret to Jean-Antoine Watteau, with whom he developed a close stylistic affinity. In 1719 he was elected to membership in the Royal Academy of Painting and Sculpture as a painter of *fêtes galantes*, a category created two years earlier for Watteau. Lancret participated in the Exposition de la Jeunesse from 1722 to 1725, and exhibited regularly at the official Salons from 1737. He received a number of royal commissions (including decorations for the Château de la Muette, the Louvre and Versailles) and enjoyed the patronage of many prominent amateurs, including Frederick II of Prussia. Lancret gradually evolved an individual style, more decorative but less poetic and symbolic than Watteau's. Although he produced portraits and history paintings, his work was devoted primarily to aristocratic genre scenes — outdoor gatherings with themes of the dance, music, the hunt and elegant repasts. Lancret's charming works are a perfect reflection of the spirit and customs of eighteenth-century French society.

33
End of the Hunt.   *c.*1740

34
Breakfast before the Hunt.   *c.*1740

The early provenance of these lunettes (from a suite of four overdoors) is elusive. They have been traditionally described as decorations from the Château de Marly, and as the Lancret pastorals backed to four Boucher panels that were made into a folding screen acquired by Lord Hertford at a Paris sale in 1851. However, there is no proof. According to John Ingamells, Director of the Wallace Collection, the paintings were listed in Lord Hertford's Paris inventory of 1871, when his estate was inherited by his son, Richard Wallace. They were installed at Bagatelle, a pavilion in the Bois de Boulogne, until Sir John Murray Scott, Lady Wallace's residuary legatee, sold it to the city of Paris in 1904. The balance of their history is well documented.

Lancret was one of the first eighteenth-century artists to depict contemporary activities in a natural, anecdotal manner, rejecting the formality and pomposity of Louis XIV's official art. The genre subjects of this suite of decorative paintings have no specific iconographic link but repeat favourite motifs in the artist's oeuvre: bathers, musicians and hunters. In these two scenes of the hunt, for which there are preparatory drawings, elegant figures, fashionably dressed, are engaged in contemporary pastimes. Lancret was the most famous and successful of Watteau's imitators, and his light-hearted vignettes, with their delicacy of execution and warm colour harmonies, achieved great success with connoisseurs of the *ancien régime*.

MCS

33
oil on canvas
62.0 x 135.0 cm (lunette)
Gift of Mrs. William Hayward
52.29.2

Provenance:
Richard Seymour-Conway, 4th Marquess Hertford, Paris, before 1870; to his son Sir Richard Wallace, Paris, 1871; to Lady Wallace (née Julie Castelnau), Paris, 1890; to Sir John Murray Scott, Paris, 1897; to Lady Victoria Sackville, London, 1913; to Jacques Seligmann, Paris, 1914; to M. Knoedler & Co., Paris and New York, 1914; Morton F. Plant, New York, 1916; to Mrs William Hayward (formerly Mrs Morton F. Plant), 1917; gifts to the de Young, 1952 and 1953.

34
oil on canvas
61.0 x 133.5 cm (lunette)
Gift of Mrs. William Hayward
53.2.2

Literature:
Georges Wildenstein, *Lancret*, Paris, 1924, nos 745–6, figs 181–80; *French Paintings*, pp. 204–8, colour reprs.

Exhibited:
Paris, Hôtel de Chimay, *Exposition de l'art français sous Louis XIV et sous Louis XV*, 1888, no. 18; San Francisco, CPLH, *French Painting from the Fifteenth Century to the Present Day*, 1934, nos 38–9.

33

34

François Boucher
1703–1770

François Boucher is the quintessential artist of the rococo, a style characterized by elegance, artifice, wit and imagination. Parisian by birth, Boucher was the son of a painter. In about 1720 he entered the studio of François Le Moyne where he learned the new style, and executed drawings for the engraver Jean-François Cars. By exhibiting at the Exposition de la Jeunesse, he met the connoisseur Jean de Jullienne, who invited him to make engravings after many of Jean-Antoine Watteau's drawings. Although Boucher won the Prix de Rome in 1723, it was not until 1727 that he went to Italy to study at his own expense. There he was influenced in particular by the Venetians Veronese and Giovanni Battista Tiepolo, and by Roman painting. He returned to Paris in 1731, became a member of the Royal Academy of Painting and Sculpture in 1734, and, upon the death of Carle Vanloo, was named both director of the Academy and First Painter to the King in 1765. His most steadfast and influential patron was the Marquise de Pompadour, mistress to Louis XV, but he was inundated with commissions throughout his official career. The range of his oeuvre includes not only paintings but decorations, tapestries, stage designs, porcelains, fans and drawings, all executed with sure draughtsmanship, inexhaustible inventiveness and a rich palette of pastel colours. Boucher continued his amazing productivity until his death, in spite of the public's changing taste, the sharp criticism of Diderot and his own failing eyesight.

35
Companions of Diana. 1745

oil on canvas
117.0 x 92.0 cm (oval)
Signed and dated at lower left: *F. Boucher/1745*
Roscoe and Margaret Oakes Collection
75.2.3

Provenance:
Perhaps sale, Paris, Hôtel des Ventes Mobilières, 28–29 November 1834, no. 15; acquired by Gregory Williams Gregory, Harlaxton Manor, Grantham, Lincolnshire; by family descent to Major Philip Pearson-Gregory, 1935 (his sale, London, Christie's, 18 June 1937, no. 12); acquired by Duveen Brothers, New York, with Wildenstein & Co.; Roscoe and Margaret Oakes, San Francisco, 1954; gift to TFAMSF, 1975.

Literature:
Royal Cortissoz, *Decorations by François Boucher*, New York, 1944, pl. 15; Regina S. Slatkin, *François Boucher in North American Collections: 100 Drawings*, exh. cat., Washington, DC, and Chicago, 1973, mentioned under no. 48, fig. 25; Alexandre Ananoff with Daniel Wildenstein, *François Boucher*, Paris, 1976, vol. 1, no. 290, fig. 846; Alexandre Ananoff, *L'opera completa di Boucher*, Milan, 1980, no. 300, repr.; Alastair Laing, *François Boucher, 1703–1770*, exh. cat., New York, 1986, mentioned under nos 49–50, fig. 153; *French Paintings*, pp. 114–16, colour repr.

36
Bacchantes. *c.*1745

These two paintings belong to a set of four overdoors from a suite of five pastoral scenes, all signed and three dated 1745, that tradition claims were commissioned by the Marquise de Pompadour and placed in her Château de Bellevue. However, Boucher was not working for Pompadour as early as 1745, and there is no trace of these pictures in the complete descriptions and inventories of Bellevue and Pompadour's estate. The oval canvases are first documented in the collection of Gregory Gregory of Harlaxton Manor, Lincolnshire. The size, opulence and fantasy of this Victorian Jacobean mansion, begun about 1831, are staggering. Gregory scoured Europe for furnishings, and these paintings, displayed in elaborate gilt-and-white Georgian frames, formed part of Harlaxton's decoration. The suite remained there until 1937.

Eighteenth-century artists used classical mythology to celebrate the glory of love and to produce charming fables that created an air of make-believe in aristocratic residences. Voluptuous womanhood was replaced with slender, girlish forms. The traditional attributes assigned to the heroes and heroines of mythology were mixed with accessories chosen according to the decorative requirements of the setting. For this beguiling suite of beauties, Boucher selected *Companions of Diana* (the huntress), *Bacchantes* (or musicians), *Pomona* (goddess of fruit) and *Flora* (with her flowers). The fifth, horizontal, pastoral is entitled *The Love Letter.* The artist's consummate skill and imagination are evident in the treatment of landscape and still life and in the brilliant effects of light and colour. Boucher made a beautiful drawing of the reclining nymph in *Companions of Diana*, which was subsequently engraved, and several copies of this painting testify to the success of the composition.

MCS

oil on canvas
117.0 x 97.0 cm
Signed at middle right: *F. Bouch[er]*
Roscoe and Margaret Oakes Collection
75.2.2

Provenance:
Same as for *Companions of Diana.*

Literature:
Royal Cortissoz, *Decorations by François Boucher,* New York, 1944, pl. 8; Alexandre Ananoff with Daniel Wildenstein, *François Boucher,* Paris, 1976, vol. 1, no. 288, fig. 843; Alexandre Ananoff, *L'opera completa di Boucher,* Milan, 1980, no. 298, repr.; Alastair Laing, 'Boucher et la pastorale peinte', *Revue de l'art,* no. 73 (1986), pp. 60, 63 n. 69, fig. 14; *French Paintings,* pp. 117–19, colour repr.

37
Virgin and Child. *c.*1765–70

All the charm and painterly qualities of Boucher's late work are evident in this small oval painting. Although at first glance it may appear to be simply a genre scene of mother and child, the traditional iconography for the Virgin Mary is represented. The rose is associated with the Virgin, and the concept of *Santa Maria della rosa*, where either the Virgin or the infant Christ holds a rose, appears early in Italian painting. In the convention of the *Mater amabilis*, the Virgin is shown half-length, wearing a red robe under a blue cloak. The warm, rich colour tones and tender poses of the figures create an intimate devotional image. Boucher attempted religious subjects throughout his career. However, critics have not always taken them seriously, finding his Madonnas too worldly and his treatment too casual.

The existence of a slightly larger painting of similar composition (in which the Virgin holds two roses), signed and dated 1768 (Germany, private collection), has created some confusion in tracing the provenance of the San Francisco picture. The popular motif of the Virgin with a rose appears again with some variations in *Returning from Market*, 1767 (Boston, Museum of Fine Arts), *Education of the Virgin*, 1768 (Phoenix Art Museum), and a sheet of drawings engraved by Gilles Demarteau after Boucher.

MCS

oil on canvas
43.0 x 35.0 cm (oval)
Signed at lower right: *F. Boucher PX* (partially effaced)
Gift of Brooke Postley
57.2

Provenance:
Probably La Ferté sale, Paris, 20 February 1797, no. 91; acquired by J.-B.-P. Le Brun, Paris; Gérard sale, Paris, 22–23 February 1850, no. 40; René A. Trotti, Paris, early twentieth century; Brooke Postley, Stamford, Connecticut; gift to the de Young, 1957.

Literature:
André Michel, *François Boucher*, Paris, 1906, no. 740; Alexandre Ananoff with Daniel Wildenstein, *François Boucher*, Paris, 1976, vol. 2, no. 662, fig. 1732; Alexandre Ananoff, *L'opera completa di Boucher*, Milan, 1980, no. 700, repr.; *French Paintings*, pp. 110–13, colour repr.

Exhibited:
Memorial Art Gallery of the University of Rochester; New Brunswick, New Jersey, The Jane Vorhees Zimmerli Art Museum, Rutgers University; Atlanta, High Museum, *La Grande Manière: Historical and Religious Painting in France, 1700–1800*, 1987–88, no. 5, repr.

Charles-André (Carle) Vanloo
1705–1765

Carle Vanloo achieved immense fame and enjoyed a brilliant career in eighteenth-century France. He is the most famous member of a successful dynasty of painters of Dutch origin. Born in Nice, Vanloo followed his brother Jean-Baptiste to Turin, and then in 1712 to Rome, where Carle studied under Benedetto Luti and the sculptor Pierre Legros. In 1724 he won the Prix de Rome, and in 1727 he arrived at the French Academy in Rome, as did his future rival François Boucher. Vanloo returned to Turin in 1732 and in 1734 was back in Paris, where he was elected to membership as a history painter in the Royal Academy of Painting and Sculpture. He rose rapidly in the hierarchy of the Academy, was ennobled in 1751, and named First Painter to the King in 1762. His patrons included members of the court, the Gobelins factory, private individuals and the church. His oeuvre includes every category: religion, history, mythology, portraiture, allegory and genre scenes. Baron Grimm called him the greatest painter in Europe, and Voltaire compared him to Raphael. In the ensuing centuries, Vanloo's critical fortune has plummeted, although his ability remains admirable, and the quality and variety of his work command respect.

38–41
Allegories of the Arts.   1753

These four allegorical paintings, together with *Comedy and Tragedy* (Moscow, Pushkin Museum of Fine Arts), were commissioned in 1752 by the Marquise de Pompadour as overdoors for the Salon de Compagnie in her newly constructed Château de Bellevue. They were exhibited at the Salon of 1753, enjoyed extraordinary success, and were copied in a wide variety of media.

In spite of minor discrepancies in dimensions throughout their provenance, the paintings in this suite have been accepted as the originals because of their quality of execution, the fact that they are the only signed versions, and because the visible previously rounded upper corners of the canvases mirror the shield-shaped engravings by Etienne Fessard after Vanloo, which were exhibited at the Salon of 1756. In addition, *Architecture* is unique in displaying the facade of Bellevue.

The novelty of the paintings lies in the use of children in fancy dress engaged in artistic pursuits, a motif that became popular in the eighteenth century. These children wear colourful costumes from the age of Louis XIV as well as from the Renaissance. It has been traditionally supposed that Madame de Pompadour, a passionate and talented amateur, was the artist's inspiration for both the painter's model and the young harpsichordist, while a bust of Louis XV is the focus of the youthful sculptor's labours. Although surely intended to flatter, these works' primary purpose was to provide a charming, amusing and original decor for Vanloo's influential patron.

MCS

Provenance:
Mme de Pompadour, Château de Bellevue, 1753; Hôtel de Pompadour, Paris, after 1757; to the Marquis de Marigny, 1764 (estate sale, Marquis de Ménars (formerly Marigny), Paris, 18 March 1782, no. 124); acquired by Basan; perhaps Frank Hall Standish, England, before 1842; bequeathed to King Louis Philippe of France, 1842 (his sale, London, Christie's, 28–30 May 1853, nos 190–3); acquired by Samuel Wheeler (his sale, London, Christie's, 29 July 1871, no. 118); bought by G. Smith; perhaps anonymous sale, London, Christie's, 21 July 1888, no. 57; bought by Speakman; perhaps anonymous sale, London, Christie's, 1 December 1888, no. 66; bought by Radley; perhaps Sir Hume Campbell (his sale, London, Christie's, 16 June 1894, nos 13–14); probably Baron

Nathaniel de Rothschild, Vienna, before 1903; confiscated by Nazi Germany, World War II, and placed in the salt mine at Alt-Aussee, Austria; returned to Alphonse de Rothschild, 1946; Rosenberg & Stiebel, New York, 1950; purchased by the CPLH, 1950.

Literature:
Pierre Rosenberg and M.-C. Sahut, *Carle Vanloo*, exh. cat., Nice, 1977, nos 125–8, reprs; *French Paintings*, pp. 292–306, colour reprs.

Exhibited:
Paris, Salon of 1753, no. 180;
The Toledo Museum of Art; The Art Institute of Chicago; Ottawa, The National Gallery of Canada, *The Age of Louis XV: French Painting, 1710–1774*, 1975–76, no. 107, pl. 83 (*Painting*).

38 *Painting*
oil on canvas
87.5 x 84.0 cm
Signed at lower left: *Carle Vanloo*
Mildred Anna Williams Collection
1950.9

39 *Sculpture*
oil on canvas
87.5 x 84.0 cm
Signed at lower right: *Carle Vanloo*
Mildred Anna Williams Collection
1950.10

40 *Architecture*
oil on canvas
87.5 x 84.0 cm
Signed at lower centre: *Carle Vanloo*
Mildred Anna Williams Collection
1950.11

41 *Music*
oil on canvas
37.5 x 84.0 cm
signed at lower centre: *Carle Vanloo*
Mildred Anna Williams Collection
1950.12

Claude-Joseph Vernet
1714–1789

Claude-Joseph Vernet, the son of a decorative painter in Avignon, was the father of Carle Vernet and the grandfather of Horace Vernet. He studied with Philippe Sauvan, a history painter, and later with Jacques Vialy in Aix-en-Provence, where a local nobleman was impressed with his talent and in 1734 sent him to Italy. There he may have studied under Adrien Manglard, a marine and landscape specialist, but he was also influenced by the seventeenth-century masters of landscape, Claude Lorrain, Gaspard Dughet and Salvator Rosa. During his stay in Rome, Vernet explored the Italian countryside, making studies after nature in Naples, Tivoli and around the lakes of Nemi and Albano. He had an international clientele by 1740, was elected a member of the Academy of Saint Luke in 1743, and began to exhibit at the Paris Salons in 1746. He returned to Paris in 1753, was elected to membership in the Royal Academy of Painting and Sculpture and, through the efforts of the Marquis de Marigny, the Superintendent of Royal Buildings and the brother of Madame de Pompadour, received a prestigious royal commission to paint a series of the ports of France (Paris, Musée du Louvre and Musée de la Marine). By 1765 he had completed fifteen canvases, remarkable for their topographical accuracy and indefatigable imagination, and all replete with numerous figures to integrate nature into the human sphere. Upon his return to Paris, Vernet was given lodgings at the Louvre and received wide critical acclaim, especially from Diderot, who preferred his work to that of Claude. Vernet's repertory includes views of ports, imaginary seascapes at sunrise and sunset, storms, shipwrecks and landscapes — all characterized by clarity of vision and mellow lighting.

42
The Bathers.   1786

In France during the early years of the eighteenth century, landscape was rarely a theme in itself, and no painter devoted his work solely to that subject. Rather than describing natural scenes, rococo artists created fantasy, for which there was a strong demand. Vernet emerges as one of the first eighteenth-century artists to revive the landscape tradition, perpetuating the Claudian vision of an ideal Italy. His style, however, was far more realistic and contemporary than the master's. In actuality, this type of art was designed especially for the British on the Grand Tour who were desirous of taking home a memento of their travels (as we do postcards).

In his later works, such as this painting, Vernet reverted not only to a familiar theme but to a more decorative formula, creating landscapes from memory in his studio. *The Bathers* represents a long and popular tradition in his work, deriving directly from the canvas in the Musée des Beaux-Arts, Nîmes. This composition was disseminated widely through engravings and was frequently copied. In this imaginary Mediterranean seaside scene, the artist conveys the tactile delight of the bathers, the golden warmth of the sun, and the refreshing coolness of the water and evokes a lingering nostalgia for the beauty and sensuality of the Mediterranean coast.

MCS

oil on canvas
57.0 x 81.0 cm
Signed and dated at lower right: *J. Vernet/f.1786*
Gift of Mrs. Georgia Worthington
76.29

Provenance:
M. M.*** sale, Paris, 20 March 1787, no. 214; Le Brun sale, Paris, 2–11 February 1813, no. 299, bought in;

Ravel collection, Lyon; sale, London, Sotheby's, 12 December 1973, no. 108; acquired by R. Green; Gerlach & Co., Amsterdam, 1973–76; purchased for the de Young, 1976.

Literature:
Florence Ingersoll-Smouse, *Joseph Vernet*, Paris, 1926, no. 1151; *French Paintings*, pp. 308–10, colour repr.

Joseph-Siffred (or Siffrein) Duplessis
1725–1802

Joseph Duplessis, as a southerner from Carpentras, near Avignon, was trained quite differently from contemporaneous court painters. As a result, recognition of his talent by Parisian society was slow to materialize. At the age of twenty he went to Rome and entered the studio of Pierre Subleyras, where he rapidly developed his artistic abilities. In 1752 he was in Paris, but it was not until 1764 that he had his first success at the Academy of Saint Luke. He achieved fame with ten works exhibited at the Salon of 1769 and was elected to membership as a portraitist by the Royal Academy of Painting and Sculpture in 1774. When he was named official court painter to Louis XVI, the aristocracy and most of the famous people of the time clamoured to sit for him. The Revolution deprived him of patrons, and he retired to Carpentras during the Reign of Terror. Back in Paris in 1796, he was appointed curator of the collections at Versailles. Recognized as the finest realistic portraitist of his generation, rivalled only by Alexandre Roslin, Duplessis recorded facial expression with a searching and sensitive brush, interpreted the moods and feelings of his sitters, and always presented clear evidence of their social position.

43
Portrait of a Gentleman
(Jean-Baptiste-François Dupré?). c.1781

In 1913 Jules Belleudy, author of the only catalogue raisonné of Duplessis's oeuvre, calls the sitter in this portrait 'unknown'. By 1920 he had become the Marquis de Chillon, and in 1931 he was named André Dupré de Billy. However, there is no firm foundation for either of these identifications. In recent years, several French claimants have asserted their ancestry with this gentleman, but these claims are unsupported by conclusive proof. The most probable suggestion is that the sitter may be Maître Jean-Baptiste-François Dupré (1747–1837), a Paris notary and counsellor to the King.

Eighteenth-century portraits are remarkable as speaking likenesses of their sitters. In this tradition, the presumed Maître Dupré, dressed in sober elegance befitting a man of law, sits at his desk, pen in hand, greeting an imaginary visitor to his well-appointed study. The furnishings of the room, meticulously reproduced by the artist, are a heterogeneous mixture of Louis XV and Louis XVI styles. In depicting the character of his sitter, the artist uses full-bodied flesh tints and strong reds, which, although not particularly flattering, give him a forceful presence. The keenness of observation, attention to detail, and brilliant rendering of materials, combined with the device of a mirror to introduce another dimension within the painting, are typical of Duplessis's talent and skill.

MCS

oil on canvas
147.0 x 114.0 cm
Mildred Anna Williams Collection
1966.46

Provenance:
Perhaps Comte d'Arjuzon, Paris; Wildenstein & Co., Paris, c.1913; purchased for the CPLH, 1966.

Literature:
Jules Belleudy, *J.-S. Duplessis, peintre du roi, 1725–1802*, Paris, 1913, pp. 340–1, no. f (as Unknown); *French Paintings*, pp. 157–9, colour repr.

Exhibited:
New York, Wildenstein & Co., *Portraits of the French Eighteenth Century*, 1923, no. V, repr. (as *Marquis de Chillon*);
New York, Wildenstein & Co., *French Eighteenth-Century Paintings*, 1948, no. 12, repr. (as *Presumed Portrait of André Dupré de Billy*);
Paris, Grand Palais; The Detroit Institute of Arts; New York, The Metropolitan Museum of Art, *French Painting, 1774–1830: The Age of Revolution*, 1974–75, no. 54, repr. p. 63.

Jean-Baptiste-Henri Deshays, called Deshays de Colleville
1729–1765

Jean-Baptiste Deshays enjoyed a brief, but brilliant, career; he was extolled by Diderot as 'the first painter of the nation' (*Salon of 1761*). Born in Colleville, near Rouen, he spent his formative years in Normandy. He studied first with his father, a minor painter, subsequently receiving instruction in drawing from Collin de Vermont, in religious painting from Jean Restout, and in the rococo style from François Boucher. He won the Prix de Rome in 1751 but spent the next three years in the studio of Carle Vanloo before taking up residence at the French Academy in Rome, then under the direction of Charles Natoire. Deshays returned to Paris in 1758, married the elder daughter of Boucher, and was made a full member of the Royal Academy of Painting and Sculpture in 1759. He exhibited at only four official Salons, on each occasion to extraordinary acclaim. Deshays's rich imagination and powers of expression were inspired by the great history painters of the seventeenth century: Eustache Le Sueur, Charles Le Brun, Peter Paul Rubens and the Carracci. The majority of his oeuvre is made up of religious and mythological compositions, conceived in the grand French decorative tradition.

44
The Abduction of Helen. c.1761

Although this painting was attributed to Boucher when acquired by the Museums, the studies of Marc Sandoz have been particularly helpful in revealing Deshays's authorship.

Greek mythology tells the tale of the abduction of the beautiful Helen, wife of Menelaus, king of Sparta, by Paris of Troy. In spite of a strong iconographic tradition in literature and the arts, the story is not chronicled in Homer's *Iliad* but mentioned only by allusion in book three. This is the subject, however, of Deshays's oil sketch in preparation for the first tapestry cartoon of the series *Iliade d'Homère*, undertaken by the Beauvais factory in 1761 and woven three times by royal command. When the sketch is compared with the tapestry, it is clear that the actual *modèle* from which the weavers worked has been lost. As is customary, the design is reversed in the tapestry, but the number of figures has been reduced, Helen now looks away from Paris, and many details have been modified or removed.

The inspiration for this composition may come from Peter Paul Rubens's Marie de Médicis cycle of 1622–25 (Paris, Musée du Louvre), a series of allegorical paintings glorifying the life of the Queen of France. The cycle was installed in the Luxembourg Palace during the eighteenth century, and the Flemish master's subject matter and use of colour exerted a profound influence on the emerging artists of the rococo. Deshays's sketch appears to share many baroque compositional motifs with *The Birth of Marie de Médicis*, especially the placement and swirling movement of the figures, and the architectural details. Although Deshays revived the heroic subjects, artistic force and sublime taste of the splendid century, his subtle, warm palette and the vivacity, ease and freedom of his brushwork anticipate Eugène Delacroix and the nineteenth century.

MCS

oil on canvas
54.0 x 87.0 cm
Gift of Rudolf J. Heinemann
54.4

Provenance:
Deshays collection, Paris, 1761 (his sale, Paris, 26 March 1765, no. 113); acquired by Abbé Gruel; Rudolf

J. Heinemann, New York, before 1953; gift to the de Young, 1954 (as by Boucher).

Literature:
Marc Sandoz, *Jean-Baptiste Deshays, 1729–1765*, Paris, 1978, pp. 84, 135, 150, no. 70–4Bb, pl. IV; *French Paintings*, pp. 152–6, colour repr.

Anne Vallayer-Coster
1744–1818

One of the most celebrated painters of eighteenth-century France, Anne Vallayer was the daughter of a goldsmith who worked for the Gobelins tapestry factory. When she was ten, her father moved his family to Paris, where he set up his own shop. Little is known of Vallayer's formal training, but she must have been exposed to a wide range of artistic expertise. Gabriel de Saint-Aubin and Jean-Baptiste-Marie Pierre, later First Painter to the King, were family friends. Vallayer's first recorded work is a portrait executed in 1762 (now lost). In 1770 she was unanimously accepted for membership in the Royal Academy of Painting and Sculpture. Although she painted some portraits, genre subjects and miniatures, it is as a productive and versatile still-life painter that she is most admired. Throughout her life Vallayer-Coster attracted the support of powerful patrons and fellow artists, and Diderot was an enthusiastic admirer. She married a wealthy lawyer and member of parliament, Jean-Pierre-Silvestre Coster, in 1781, the same year she was given an apartment at the Louvre. She last exhibited at the Salon of 1817. While her work is undeniably comparable in style and subject matter with that of Jean-Baptiste-Siméon Chardin, Vallayer-Coster was not merely an agile imitator. Her continuing influence may be seen in the work of such nineteenth-century still-life painters as François Bonvin and Henri Fantin-Latour.

45
Still Life with Plums and a Lemon. 1778

This beautiful painting is a perfect example of the austere and serene still-life compositions for which Vallayer-Coster is well known. She treated the motif of a basket of plums frequently and with little variation, always concentrating on the outline of each object, its texture, and the subtle harmonies of a sombre palette. The simple presentation of familiar household objects is a type of still life that originated in the Low Countries in the early seventeenth century and was introduced into France by Louise Moillon, Lubin Baugin and others. Chardin revived the formula in the 1730s, and Vallayer-Coster followed his example, finding steady patronage from bourgeois clients for these traditional works. There is another, rectangular version of this painting in a private collection in New York. In addition, the artist used the same basket of plums in a still life now in Cleveland (see Marianne Roland Michel, 'A Basket of Plums', *The Bulletin of the Cleveland Museum of Art* 60 (February 1973), pp. 52–9).

Chardin had used the same motif in *Still Life with Plums*, c.1730 (New York, The Frick Collection). However, while both artists are superb colourists, Vallayer-Coster's interpretation is more specific and more freely painted, less mysterious and perhaps more appealing.

MCS

oil on canvas
41.5 x 47.5 cm
Signed and dated at lower right: *Mlle Vallayer/1778*
Gift of Mr. and Mrs. Louis A. Benoist
1960.30

Provenance:
A. Weinberger; to Harry G. Sperling, New York, 1958; purchased by the CPLH, 1960.

Literature:
Marianne Roland Michel, *Anne Vallayer-Coster,*

1744–1818, Paris, 1970, no. 138, repr.; *French Paintings*, pp. 284–7, colour repr.

Exhibited:
Perhaps Paris, Salon of 1779, no. 105;
Los Angeles County Museum of Art; Austin, University Art Museum, The University of Texas; Pittsburgh, Museum of Art, Carnegie Institute; New York, The Brooklyn Museum, *Women Artists, 1550–1950,* 1976–77, no. 55, repr.

A pupil of both Jacques-Augustin Silvestre, drawing master to the royal children of France, and Joseph-Marie Vien, a neoclassical painter, Etienne Aubry began his career as a portraitist. He exhibited several portraits, including one of Etienne Jeaurat, in his debut at the official Salon of 1771. Accepted as a full member of the Royal Academy of Painting and Sculpture in 1775, he turned increasingly toward the genre painting for which he is best known. A fine colourist, he was inspired by Jean-Baptiste Greuze's moralizing subject matter and by Jean-Honoré Fragonard's handling of paint. In 1777 he travelled to Rome to study at the French Academy under the auspices of the Comte d'Angivillier, his most important patron. However, his ambition to be a history painter was not successful, and he returned to France in 1780. His final attempt at the grand manner was exhibited posthumously at the Salon of 1781 (*Coriolanus' Farewell to His Wife before Leaving to Give Himself up to the Volsii* (now lost)). Aubry's originality is most apparent in his portraiture, which is characterized by a robust technique and psychological insight. His portraits of the aristocracy tend to be more formal and restrained than the intimate, even affectionate, likenesses of his fellow artists, such as Noël Hallé and Louis-Claude Vassé (both Château de Versailles).

46
Etienne Jeaurat. 1771

The attribution of this painting posed a problem for many years, but the identity of the sitter has always been certain. Etienne Jeaurat (1699–1789) was a popular genre painter who exhibited frequently at the official Salons. He also had a great success in the hierarchy of the Royal Academy of Painting and Sculpture. Several likenesses of Jeaurat attributed to various artists are known, but none of them are signed. Although Jeaurat himself was a creditable painter, none of his known works are the equal of this brilliant portrait, in spite of his family's claims (Puychevrier, p. 27).

For many years this portrait, as well as *Christoph W. Gluck* (Paris, Musée du Louvre), with which it shares many stylistic similarities, was given to Greuze. However, the precision of treatment here is noticeably different from that of Greuze's portrait *Etienne Jeaurat* (Paris, Musée du Louvre), which was exhibited at the Salon of 1769. In addition, it would have been extremely unusual for Greuze to paint two different portraits of the same person within two years.

Edgar Munhall, a leading Greuze scholar, has long refuted the attribution to Greuze, believing that this is the 'lost' portrait of Jeaurat by Aubry, exhibited at the Salon of 1771. The quality of this vivacious likeness, skilfully composed and beautifully painted, was favourably noticed by contemporary critics. The Munhall attribution is consistent with all the evidence compiled to date, and the painting is now generally accepted as one of Aubry's major works.

MCS

oil on canvas
91.0 x 73.0 cm
Roscoe and Margaret Oakes Collection
75.2.1

Provenance:
Etienne Jeaurat (estate inventory of 1789); by family descent to Mme Nicolas-François Richer, before 1862; Noël Bardac, Paris, 1910; Colonel and Mme Jacques Balsan, Paris, *c.*1924; Arnold Seligmann Rey & Co., Paris, *c.*1934; Rosenberg & Stiebel, New York, 1953; to Roscoe and Margaret Oakes, San Francisco, 1953; gift to TFAMSF, 1975 (as by Greuze).

Literature:
Sylvain Puychevrier, *Le Peintre Etienne Jeaurat: Essai*

historique et biographique sur cet artiste, Paris, 1862, pp. 27, 32; Max Osborn, *Die Kunst des Rokoko*, Berlin, 1929, no. 218, repr. (as by Greuze); *French Paintings*, pp. 105–8, colour repr.

Exhibited:
Probably Paris, Salon of 1771, no. 266;
Berlin, Académie Royale des Arts, *Exposition d'oeuvres de l'art français au XVIIIème siècle*, 1910, no. 58, repr. (as by Greuze);
Indianapolis, Herron Museum of Art, *The Romantic Era: Birth and Flowering, 1750–1850*, 1965, no. 3, repr. (as by Greuze);
Bordeaux, Musée des Beaux-Arts, *La Peinture française: Collections américaines*, 1966, no. 27 (as by Greuze).

Jacques-Louis David
1748–1825

Born in Paris to a family of masons and building contractors, Jacques-Louis David studied under Joseph-Marie Vien, to whom he had been recommended by François Boucher, a relative by marriage. After receiving the Prix de Rome in 1774 on his fourth attempt, David spent five years at the French Academy in Italy. Immersion in the art of the ancients and the old masters had a reformative impact on his style, and he abandoned the colourism of his early rococo manner for a more monumental and sombre approach. With *The Grief of Andromache* of 1783 (Paris, Ecole des Beaux-Arts), he was elected to the Royal Academy of Painting and Sculpture, and his *Oath of the Horatii* of 1784–85 (Paris, Musée du Louvre) became a manifesto for the new classicism. David played a major role in the French Revolution, serving on the Committee for Public Instruction, organizing political pageants and working on such revolutionary images as *The Oath of the Tennis Court* (Château de Versailles) and *Death of Marat* (Brussels, Musée des Beaux-Arts). After the fall of Robespierre, he was arrested and imprisoned for a short time. David rose to power again, however, through his support of Napoleon, for whom he painted numerous portraits and grand commemorative pictures such as *The Coronation of Napoleon and Josephine*, 1806–07 (Paris, Musée du Louvre). With the Bourbon Restoration, David was forced into exile in Brussels, where he maintained a studio and attempted in his late portraits and mythologies a reconciliation between drawing and colour, and realism and idealism.

47
Laure-Emilie-Félicité David, Baronne Meunier. 1812

While at the height of his fame as leader of the neoclassical school in France and First Painter to Napoleon, David undertook between 1810 and 1813 a series of portraits of members of his family, all in the same half-length format. The painting of his wife, Marguerite-Charlotte David, is dated 1813 and is now in the National Gallery of Art, Washington, DC. A portrait from 1810 of Baron Jeanin, one of David's two sons-in-law, recently resurfaced in a private collection in Europe, and another of Baron Meunier, his other son-in-law, has disappeared. The well-known, unfinished portraits of his twin daughters, Baronne Laure-Emilie-Félicité Meunier and Baronne Pauline Jeanin, are now in San Francisco and in the Sammlung Oskar Reinhart, Winterthur, respectively. The date of 1812 for the former is based on the catalogue of David's work by his grandson Jacques-Louis-Jules David.

The David twins were born on 26 October 1786 in Paris and baptized the next day at the church of Saint-Germain-l'Auxerrois. Emilie grew up to be the more tranquil and reserved of the two, qualities of personality discernible in the quiet warmth of her father's portrayal. In 1805 she married Claude-Marie Meunier (1770–1846), who had distinguished himself in military service during several campaigns in the Napoleonic Wars. He was awarded the Legion of Honour in 1806, the title Baron of the Empire in 1808, and the rank of brigade general in 1810.

It is not known why the two portraits of the artist's daughters remain unfinished. They feature a loose, sketchy touch, thin transparencies of paint, and rapidly scrubbed backgrounds reminiscent of David's famous unfinished portraits from his Revolutionary and earlier Napoleonic periods — works such as *Mme Trudaine* and *Mme Récamier* (both Paris, Musée du Louvre). Already in the painting of Emilie, however, certain traits are apparent that would characterize David's style during his exile in Brussels after 1815; these include the mannerisms of anatomy based on Greek vase painting, and a generally brighter palette. Here the strong contrast of undiluted vermilion in the velvet dress and orange-yellow in the chair provides a dazzling colouristic note that may have helped convince David to leave the picture in its present state.

SAN

oil on canvas
73.5 x 60.0 cm
Roscoe and Margaret Oakes Collection
75.2.6

Provenance:
Family of the sitter, Calais; by descent to Mme Marius
Bianchi (née Mathilde Jeanin), by 1913; Comtesse
Joachim Murat, *c.*1930–40; Marquis de Ludre-Frolois;
to Galerie Cailleux, Paris, by 1948; M. Knoedler & Co.,
New York, 1954; to Roscoe and Margaret Oakes, San
Francisco, 1955; gift to TFAMSF, 1975.

Literature:
Jacques-Louis-Jules David, *Le Peintre David,*

1748–1825: Souvenirs et documents inédits, Paris,
1880–82, vol. 2, pp. 487, 648, repr.; Louis Hautecoeur,
Louis David, Paris, 1954, p. 230; Anita Brookner,
Jacques-Louis David, London, 1980, pp. 169–70;
Antoine Schnapper, *David, témoin de son temps*,
Fribourg, 1980, p. 266; *French Paintings*, pp. 143–7,
colour repr.

Exhibited:
Paris, Petit Palais, *David et ses élèves*, 1913, no. 54;
Paris, Musée de l'Orangerie, *David: Exposition en
l'honneur du deuxième centenaire de sa naissance*,
1948, no. 65;
Paris, Musée du Louvre, *Jacques-Louis David,
1748–1825*, 1989–90, no. 214, colour repr.

Pierre-Henri de Valenciennes
1750–1819

Born in Toulouse, Pierre-Henri de Valenciennes received his early training under Jean-Baptiste Despax, a history painter, and Guillaume-Gabriel Bouton, a miniaturist. He went to Italy in 1769 with his patron, Mathias du Bourg, was in Paris by 1771, and two years later entered the studio of the history painter Gabriel-François Doyen. During this period Valenciennes began to sketch in the French countryside. He returned to Italy in 1777, remaining there until 1784–85, with the exception of travels in Sicily and Switzerland and a visit in 1781 to Paris. There Claude-Joseph Vernet gave him instruction in perspective and encouraged his *plein-air* studies. Essentially, however, the artist appears to be self-taught as a landscape painter.

Valenciennes became a member of the Royal Academy of Painting and Sculpture in 1787 and continued to exhibit at the Salons until 1819. From 1796 to 1800 he taught courses in perspective, and in 1799–1800 published his famous treatise, *Elémens de perspective pratique à l'usage des artistes*, as well as an essay on landscape painting. In 1812 he was appointed Professor of Perspective at the Ecole des Beaux-Arts and he was awarded the Legion of Honour in 1815. The Ecole established a Prix de Rome for historical landscape in 1816.

Strongly influenced by the classical landscape tradition of Nicolas Poussin and Claude Lorrain, Valenciennes was largely responsible for elevating the status of landscape painting in the late eighteenth century. As a respected teacher and theoretician, he helped form a generation of landscape painters, including Jean-Victor Bertin and Achille-Etna Michallon, who became Camille Corot's masters.

48
A Capriccio of Rome with the Finish of a Marathon. 1788

As a landscape painter Valenciennes was inspired by the lofty ideals of the seventeenth century. He believed that the landscape artist should be highly educated and skilled, and the theories he espouses in his *Elémens* were meant to instruct his young students. Classifying three types of landscape, he describes the highest form, *paysage historique*, as an idealized view of nature with a specific subject from mythology or an ancient text. Second is *paysage pastoral*, which also presents an idealized view of nature, but the subject matter is non-literary. Third are *vues*, or realistic depictions of nature and its effects. Initially sketched outdoors, Valenciennes's own *vues* had a strong influence on nineteenth-century landscapists.

This *paysage pastoral*, exhibited for the first time in 1789, follows precisely Valenciennes's theories of composition. The carefully delineated foreground, middle ground and background all recede into space in a measured rhythm. Two masses of foliage on either side provide a framing device for the pictorial space. The canvas is highly finished, displaying a subtle and harmonious palette, with a careful balance of tones and values. There are only a few touches of bright colour. The scene is animated by a foot race outside the walls of a *capriccio* of Rome. A drawing at the Matthiesen Gallery, London (as of 1987), which was executed by Valenciennes in Italy, may be a preparatory study for the background scene at the left. Thoughtful and deliberate in conception and execution, this beautiful painting ranks with the best neoclassical landscapes of the French revolutionary era.

MCS

oil on canvas
81.0 x 119.0 cm
Signed and dated at lower centre: *P. devalenciennes pinxit/1788*
Museum purchase, Roscoe and Margaret Oakes Income Fund and Art Trust Fund
1983.28

Provenance:
Marquis de Clermont d'Amboise, by 1789 (his sale, Paris, Hôtel de Bullion, 20 May 1790, no. 35); acquired by Demarest, Paris; Emerich Joseph, Duke of Dalberg, Herrnsheim, *c*.1790; to his daughter, Marie-Louise Pellini, Lady F. R. E. Dalberg-Acton, 1833; to her son John Emerich Edward, 1st Baron Acton, 1837; Baron Cornelius von Heyl zu Herrnsheim, 1884 (by purchase of Schloss Herrnsheim from Lord Acton); by family descent to Baron Siegfried von Heyl zu Herrnsheim (who sold the castle in 1957); to Beata Reynolds and her sister, 1982; sale, London, Sotheby's, 15 March 1983, no. 2; acquired by Stair Sainty Matthiesen, New York; purchased by TFAMSF, 1983.

Literature:
Robert Mesuret, *Pierre-Henri de Valenciennes*, exh. cat., Toulouse, 1956–57, pp. 11, 31; *French Paintings*, pp. 280–3, colour repr.

Exhibited:
Paris, Salon of 1789, no. 120;
New York, Colnaghi, *Claude to Corot: The Development of Landscape Painting in France*, 1990, no. 54, colour repr.

Elisabeth Louise Vigée Le Brun
1755–1842

Elisabeth Louise Vigée Le Brun, one of the most famous and successful French artists of the eighteenth century, was the daughter of Louis Vigée, a portraitist, pastellist and professor at the Academy of Saint Luke. Her early artistic training was in her father's studio, and she enjoyed the advice and encouragement of some of the major artists of the era, such as Claude-Joseph Vernet and Jean-Baptiste Greuze. Through access to public and private collections in Paris, she was able to study the Flemish painters, particularly Peter Paul Rubens, and the Italian masters.

At fifteen she began a brilliant career as a portraitist, attracting a large aristocratic clientele with her virtuosity, her delicate brushwork and the flattering manner in which she depicted her sitters. In 1776 she married Jean-Baptiste-Pierre Le Brun, an important and influential picture dealer, and in 1778 she was invited to portray Queen Marie Antoinette (Vienna, Kunsthistorisches Museum), thereafter becoming her official portraitist, intimate friend and confidant. At the Queen's insistence, Vigée Le Brun was admitted to membership in the Royal Academy of Painting and Sculpture in 1783, and from then until 1789 enjoyed her most productive and creative years, portraying the artistic, aristocratic and theatrical luminaries of the *ancien régime*.

She fled France at the onset of the Revolution, spending the next twelve years in exile. She travelled throughout Europe and Russia, executing numerous portraits, and was made a member of most of the academies in the capital cities of Europe. Vigée Le Brun's *Souvenirs*, published in 1835–37, chronicle her remarkable life and career.

49
Hyacinthe Gabrielle Roland, later Marchioness Wellesley. 1791

This ravishing portrait of Hyacinthe Gabrielle Roland was painted in Rome, where both the sitter and the artist sought refuge after the commencement of the French Revolution. Mademoiselle Roland was at that time the mistress of Richard Colley Wellesley, Earl of Mornington and later Marquess Wellesley (1799), the elder brother of the Duke of Wellington. Before their marriage in 1794, their union produced five children, one of whom became the great-great-grandmother of the present Queen Elizabeth II of England. Wellesley pursued an illustrious career in government service and in 1797 was appointed Governor-General of India. He remained there for eight years, leaving his family behind in England. The couple was formally separated after his return, and Marchioness Wellesley died in 1816.

An apt student of the art of the past, Vigée Le Brun found inspiration for compositional devices, poses, colour and costume in the works of Raphael, Rubens, van Dyck and the Italian seventeenth-century masters, as well as in classical sculpture. This portrait demonstrates the artist's close examination and assimilation of the fluidity and luminosity of Rubens's brushwork. The pose and rendering of the skin passages are reminiscent of Rubens's famous portrait *Hélène Fourment in a Fur Coat* (*Het Pelsken*) (Vienna, Kunsthistorisches Museum), which the artist must have known through a copy or a print. However, the simple costume, bold colour scheme of red, white and black against a rich blue background, and three-quarter pose are favourite motifs in Vigée Le Brun's work.

The beauty, vivacity and sensuality of this appealing sitter are perfectly revealed by the artist's painterly technique. While evoking the old masters, the painting also anticipates the stylistic freedom and emotionalism associated with nineteenth-century romanticism.

MCS

oil on canvas
99.0 x 75.0 cm
Signed, inscribed and dated at lower left: *L. Vigee le Brun/Roma 1791*
Mildred Anna Williams Collection, Bequest Funds of Henry S. Williams in memory of H. K. S. Williams
1991.29

Provenance:
Inherited by Hyacinthe Mary Wellesley, Lady Hatherton, 1816; Hatherton family, until the 1930s; Lord Sanderson of Ayot; sale, London, Christie's, 26 June 1964, no. 74; Duits Ltd., London, by 1965; Schaeffer Galleries, New York, by 1967; Elizabeth Parke Firestone, Newport, Rhode Island (her sale, New York, Christie's, 22 March 1991, no. 654); to Colnaghi, New York; purchased by TFAMSF, 1991.

Literature:
E. L. Vigée Le Brun, *Souvenirs*, Paris, 1835–37, vol. 2, pp. 39, 368; Clifford Duits, ed., 'Portrait of Mademoiselle Roland (Later the Marchioness Wellesley) by Madame Vigée Le Brun', *Duits Quarterly* 9 (Winter 1965), pp. 11–16, colour repr.; Joseph Baillio, 'Vigée Le Brun and the Classical Practice of Imitation', in 'Paris: Center of Artistic Enlightenment', *Papers in Art History from the Pennsylvania State University* 4 (1988), p. 102, fig. 4-25; Guy S. Sainty, *Eighty Years of French Painting: From Louis XVI to the Second Republic*, exh. cat., New York, 1991, no. 5, colour repr.

Jan-Frans van Dael
1764–1840

Flemish by origin, Jan-Frans van Dael spent most of his life in France. He first studied architecture in his native Antwerp before going to Paris in 1786. There he was commissioned to assist in the *trompe l'oeil* decorations for the châteaux of Saint Cloud, Bellevue and Chantilly. The influence of his master, Gérard van Spaendonck, was instrumental in van Dael's decision to specialize in still-life paintings of fruits and flowers, thereafter relegating interior decoration, portraits, religious subjects and landscapes to rarities in his oeuvre. He exhibited for the first time at the Salon of 1793, the same year he was given quarters at the Louvre. From 1806 to 1817 he lived at the Sorbonne as an artist protected by the State. Patronized by Louis XVIII and Charles X, as well as the empresses Josephine and Marie-Louise, van Dael was decorated as a Knight of the Legion of Honour in 1825. He was interred in the cemetery of Père Lachaise, next to his former teacher, van Spaendonck. A very successful painter who commanded high prices for his work, van Dael taught a number of students who continued the northern tradition of flower painting.

50
Flowers before a Window. 1789

Van Dael was one of the more important of the northern artists, including the van Spaendonck brothers and Pierre-Joseph Redouté, who gathered in Paris toward the end of the eighteenth century to perpetuate the Dutch tradition of flower painting. Inspired in particular by the seventeenth-century master Jan van Huysum, these artists remained faithful to their northern training while sounding a more modern, nineteenth-century note. Their style — precise, highly decorative, and almost scientific in the recording of every petal and stamen — stood in contrast to the more sombre, traditional French mode practised by such artists as Anne Vallayer-Coster.

Except in his most ambitious works, *Offering to Flora*, 1799 (now lost), and *Tomb of Julie*, 1804 (Musée National du Château de Malmaison), van Dael usually places his compositions of flowers in a simple vase on a stone table or marble ledge. This brilliant bouquet is depicted with great precision and diversity. Included in the lavish display are a number of flowers that before modern greenhouses did not bloom naturally at the same time of year, such as hyacinths and roses. As did his contemporaries, van Dael composed floral arrangements in his studio, often from previous studies. The illumination from the open window at the left enables the artist to demonstrate his skill at distributing light, shadow and colour as the viewer's eye moves from the brightness of the left to the shade of the right. The inclusion of a bird's nest with eggs and a few insects may signal the Dutch tradition of *vanitas*, or the transience of all living things.

MCS

oil on canvas
92.5 x 79.5 cm
Signed and dated at lower right: *J. Van Dael f./1789*
Mildred Anna Williams Collection
1952.79

Provenance:
Frank Partridge, London, before 1924; M. Knoedler & Co., London, July 1924; C. S. Carstairs, New York, 1925; Charles Towers (on consignment to Knoedler), 1952; purchased by the CPLH, 1952.

Literature:
Jacques Foucart, *French Painting, 1774–1830: The Age of Revolution*, exh. cat., Paris, Detroit, New York, 1974–75, p. 635 (Fr. ed.), p. 642 (Eng. ed.); *French Paintings*, pp. 288–90, colour repr.

Exhibited:
Santa Barbara Museum of Art, *Fruits and Flowers in Painting*, 1958, no. 23, repr.

Baron François Gérard
1770–1837

François Gérard was one of the most accomplished students of Jacques-Louis David to emerge during the 1790s. Best known for his portraits, he carried on the tenets of David's classical teaching into the 1830s. Gérard was born in Rome and spent his childhood in Italy, where his father served as an administrator under the French ambassador to the Holy See. After his family returned to Paris, he was apprenticed to the sculptor J.-B. Pajou and then to the painter Nicolas-Guy Brenet before entering David's studio in 1786. Gérard took second place in the Prix de Rome of 1789 but did not compete further. His illustrations for works by ancient authors published by Didot Frères helped him support his family during the Revolution. He exhibited at the Salons of 1791 and 1793 but drew particular attention for his *Belisarius* at the Salon of 1795 and for his portraits from the later 1790s. Napoleon confirmed his fame with commissions for official portraits and decorations on the theme of Ossian for his home at Malmaison, and there followed a series of large history paintings, such as *The Battle of Austerlitz* of 1810 (Château de Versailles). Commissions continued under Louis XVIII, and Gérard's *Henry IV Entering Paris* (Château de Versailles) celebrated the Bourbon Restoration. Much honoured and decorated, Gérard continued to paint until his death in 1837, although his work declined in quality after about 1830.

51
Comtesse de Morel-Vindé and Her Daughter (The Music Lesson).   1799

Even within the cool refinement and studied grandeur of his neoclassical style, Gérard has managed to produce in this work a portrait with great warmth and affection. It was commissioned in 1799 by Charles-Gilbert de Morel-Vindé (1759–1842), formerly a member of the parliament of Paris, who retired from public life in 1791 to pursue his interests in writing, agricultural research and the collecting of paintings and books. The setting is a salon in the Morel-Vindés' fashionable home in Paris, the Hôtel de Vindé, on the boulevard de la Madeleine. Gérard has taken pains to reproduce the view from their window and also to record through clothing and such details as the Empire chair their cultivated, contemporary tastes. At the left stands Mme Morel-Vindé, born Marie-Renée-Elisabeth Choppin d'Arnouville (1763–1835). Seated at the piano-forte is one of the two Morel-Vindé daughters, either Claire-Marie or Cécile-Louise: she has not been conclusively identified. She seems to have just finished a recital of the song entitled on the sheet music '*à ma mère*' and now turns to her mother for approbation. In keeping with this sentimental theme of filial piety and devotion, so much in vogue at the time, the embracing hands of the sitters form the visual and psychological centre of the painting. The daughter clutches the forearm of her mother lovingly and imploringly, while the mother's clasp of the young woman's other hand is solid and reassuring.

Gérard prevents the subject from becoming maudlin by the balance of his composition and his remarkable blending of richness and restraint. As Rosenberg and Stewart have noted: 'Great faithfulness in the rendering of the materials, an expressive and sensitive analysis of faces, extraordinary refinement of the facture, and technical virtuosity as demonstrated in the treatment of the landscape seen through the muslin curtains make this ambitious portrait a masterpiece' (*French Paintings*, p. 177).

SAN

oil on canvas
200.0 x 143.0 cm
Museum purchase, Mildred Anna Williams Collection
and William H. Noble Bequest Fund
1979.8

Provenance:
Charles-Gilbert More, Vicomte de Morel-Vindé, Paris, 1799–1842; to his granddaughter, Claudine-Renée-Christine Terray, Comtesse de Narcillac, 1843–72; to her son, Comte Ernest de Narcillac, Bellevue, 1872–1911; to his nephew, Comte Alain de Maingard, 1911; private collection; Galerie Brame et Lorenceau, Paris, c.1978; purchased by the CPLH, 1979.

Literature:
Charles Blanc, *Histoire des peintres de toutes les écoles: Ecole française*, Paris, 1862–63, vol. 3, p. 8; Baron Henri Gérard, *Lettres adressées au Baron François Gérard peintre d'histoire, par les artistes et les personnages célèbres de son temps*, Paris, 1886, vol. l, p. 9; vol. 2, p. 404; Alain Latreille, 'Catalogue raisonné des portraits peints par le baron François Gérard (1770–1837)', Mémoire de l'Ecole du Louvre, Paris, 1973, pp. 151–2, no. 126, fig. 12; *French Paintings*, pp. 174–7, colour repr.

Exhibited:
Paris, Salon of 1799, no. 716.

Unknown Artist
Eighteenth century

This small masterpiece has so far eluded all efforts to find a precise attribution or an identification of the sitter. Since 1916 the painting has been considered a self-portrait by Jean-Honoré Fragonard, but such contemporary scholars as Jacques Thuillier, Pierre Rosenberg and Jean-Pierre Cuzin have challenged that attribution on stylistic grounds. Both François-André Vincent and Louis Durameau have been suggested as possible authors of this work, but without convincing proof. In addition, there are striking similarities of treatment between the San Francisco portrait and *Bust of a Man Reading* (Zurich, Stiftung Sammlung E. G. Bührle), previously identified as a portrait of Hubert Robert. However, no firm attribution for either picture has been forthcoming.

52
Portrait of a Miniaturist

While this is certainly the portrait of a miniaturist, bent studiously over his work, holding a thin brush and small palette, who is he? Fragonard is known to have worked occasionally in miniature, but the pose of the head makes it difficult to judge the features of this sitter, and comparison with documented likenesses of Fragonard makes it impossible to accept this as his portrait (Rosenberg, 1987–88, nos 287–90, repr.).

It has been suggested that this may be a portrait of P.-A. Hall, a Swedish artist who lived in Paris around 1766 and whose self-portrait, *c.*1780 (Stockholm, private collection), bears some similarity to our sitter. The possibility of other late-eighteenth-century miniaturists being the sitter here has also been explored, but no convincing historic or iconographic evidence has been found.

The canvas has great pictorial qualities — rapid brushwork, thick impasto and bold use of colour. The sitter, dressed in a red and green robe and strongly modelled with white accents and dramatic lighting, is posed against a warm deep brown background. Although this portrait is the work of an innovative and skilful artist, scholars rejecting the Fragonard attribution find the red and green tonalities too cold, the handling too uneven and casual, and the light effects too harsh (Cuzin, p. 8). It is hoped that the names of both the artist and the miniaturist will be revealed one day.

MCS

oil on canvas
45.5 x 37.5 cm
Gift of Mr. and Mrs. Louis A. Benoist
1959.24

Provenance:
Perhaps M. R.*** sale, Paris, Hôtel Drouot, 25 March 1875, no. 53, as *Portrait of a Painter*; Jean Dollfus, Paris, by 1885 (his sale, Paris, Galerie Georges Petit, 20–21 May 1912, no. 27, as French School, *Portrait of a Miniaturist*); acquired by Wildenstein & Co., Paris; Baron Maurice de Rothschild, Paris; Judge Elbert H. Gary, New York (his sale, New York, American Art Association, 20 April 1928, no. 26, as *Self-Portrait* by Fragonard); acquired by Charles Haydon, New York; to J. W. Willard Haydon, Boston; Mrs Daniel C. Jackling, San Francisco, *c.*1952; to Mrs Robert F. Gill, San Francisco; purchased by the CPLH, 1959 (as *Self-Portrait* by Fragonard).

Literature:
Georges Wildenstein, *The Paintings of Fragonard*, London, 1960, no. 486, pl. III; Daniel Wildenstein and Gabriele Mandel, *L'opera completa di Fragonard*, Milan, 1972, no. 515, repr.; *French Paintings*, pp. 329–31, colour repr.; Pierre Rosenberg, *Fragonard*, exh. cat., Paris and New York, 1987–88, mentioned under no. 287; Jean-Pierre Cuzin, *Fragonard: Life and Work*, New York, 1988, p. 8, fig. 4; Pierre Rosenberg, *Tout l'oeuvre peint de Fragonard*, Paris, 1989, p. 134 (as rejected).

Exhibited:
Tokyo, The National Museum of Western Art; Kyoto, Municipal Museum, *Fragonard*, 1980, no. 80, repr.

Nineteenth-Century French Paintings

Théodore Géricault
1791–1824

Born in Rouen of wealthy parents, Théodore Géricault moved to Paris with his family about 1796. After studying at the Lycée Impérial, in 1808 he entered the studio of Carle Vernet, whose easygoing instruction he later quit for a stricter program of study (1810–11) under the neoclassicist Pierre Guérin. Géricault also worked on his own, copying examples in the Louvre of the dramatic art of Peter Paul Rubens, Anthony van Dyck, Titian, Veronese and others. At the Salon of 1812 he exhibited his first major independent painting, *The Charging Chasseur* (Paris, Musée du Louvre), which won a medal and announced through its fiery treatment of military valour the emergence of the artist's strongly romantic sensibility. Experiments with an antique manner preceded a trip to Italy in 1816–17. After exploring a number of themes that resulted in many small-scale works, Géricault finally found in the story of the raft of the *Medusa* a contemporary epic that allowed him to raise realism to a powerfully monumental level; his painting on the theme (Paris, Musée du Louvre) was exhibited at the Salon of 1819. In 1820–22 he lived in England, where he concentrated on genre subjects and lithographs. A series of portraits of the insane marks a final dramatic achievement. Géricault died in 1824 of a spinal disease that had been exacerbated by riding accidents.

53
after Anthony van Dyck
Equestrian Portrait of Charles V. c.1814–15

This small but dramatic oil sketch typifies Géricault's studies after old master paintings during the period 1812–15, when he rebelled against Guérin's neoclassical instruction and developed a far more bold and expressive style. The painting copied in this case is an equestrian portrait of Emperor Charles V, a work located since the seventeenth century in the Uffizi, Florence, and originally considered an autograph van Dyck, although this attribution is now questioned. More precisely, Géricault's source can be identified as an engraving by Jean-Baptiste Wicar after the van Dyck painting; the engraving, published in *Tableaux, statues, bas-reliefs, et camées de la Galerie de Florence et du Palais Pitti* (Paris, 1789), reverses the original, as does Géricault's copy. He used the same compendium of prints for numerous other studies as well. Except for his elimination of certain details, such as an eagle flying over the Emperor's head with a laurel wreath, a sash billowing behind him, and the horse's reins and bridle, Géricault has followed the print fairly faithfully. As Lorenz Eitner observes in the 1989 exhibition catalogue, however, Géricault copied such reproductive engravings 'partly, no doubt, for the sake of convenience, but perhaps also because these often rather crude reproductions allowed him some freedom of self-expression' (p. 47). Early confusions over the provenance of the San Francisco painting are clarified by Johnson (1970) and Bazin (1987), who show that it was not this picture but another copy by Géricault after van Dyck that belonged to Eugène Delacroix and figured in Ary Scheffer's collection.

Although the authenticity of the present sketch has been denied by Grunchec (1978) and Bazin (1987), neither scholar had the opportunity to examine the work in person. The removal of an old and badly discoloured varnish layer, in a cleaning in 1989, revealed a palette and stylistic handling fully consistent with Géricault's early autograph works: the visible reddish-brown ground and underdrawing in ink are characteristic technical features. The fluid impastos of the horse's mane and tail and in the sky show the extent to which the young artist's painterly skills had already developed, as does the translation of the original black and white source into a bold play of white and red against a broodingly dark background. Although the figure is somewhat wooden in modelling, it is built up in a typically sculptural manner with a few deft, thick strokes. Moreover, the theme of powerful natural forces, as manifested in the stormy sky and majestic horse, is one that would compel much of Géricault's best work throughout the remainder of his career.

SAN

oil on canvas
45.8 x 37.5 cm
Memorial gift from Dr. T. Edward and Tullah Hanley,
Bradford, Pennsylvania
69.30.219

Provenance:
Samuel P. Avery, New York; Charles Stewart Smith (his
sale, New York, American Art Association, 4 January
1935, no. 35); Julius H. Weitzner, Inc., New York, by
1936; Dr T. Edward and Tullah Hanley, Bradford,
Pennsylvania, by 1952; gift to the de Young, 1969.

Literature:
Klaus Berger, *Géricault und sein Werk*, Vienna, 1952,
p. 79, no. 1, repr.; Lee Johnson, 'A Copy after Van
Dyck by Géricault', *Burlington Magazine* 113, no. 813
(December 1970), p. 794; Jacques Thuillier and
Philippe Grunchec, *L'opera completa di Géricault*,
Milan, 1978, no. A68, repr.; Germain Bazin, *Théodore
Géricault: Etude critique, documents, et catalogue
raisonné*, Paris, 1987, vol. 2, pp. 300, 446, no. 346,
repr.

Exhibited:
New York, Julius H. Weitzner, Inc., *A Selection of
Paintings*, 1936, no. 35, repr.;
San Francisco, CPLH, *Géricault, 1791–1824*, 1989, p. 8
n. 5, no. 11, colour repr. p. 21.

Jean-Baptiste-Camille Corot
1796–1875

Jean-Baptiste-Camille Corot was born in Paris, the son of a milliner. After apprenticing with a draper, he was allowed by his parents to pursue his ambitions in art, and from 1822 to 1824 he studied landscape painting with Achille-Etna Michallon and Jean-Victor Bertin. In the classical tradition, he went to Italy to study in 1825 and remained there for three years, painting together with Théodore-Caruelle d'Aligny and working mostly out of doors on oil sketches. Here he developed the serene, fresh landscape style that became his hallmark, although he continued throughout his life to produce paintings for the Salons in a more traditional and classical vein. Corot returned to Italy in 1834 and 1843 and also travelled to Switzerland, Holland and England. Although he exhibited regularly at the Salon from 1827, he achieved critical success and official patronage only in the later 1840s and 1850s. He was awarded the Legion of Honour in 1846. In the early 1850s, Corot's work underwent a transformation from sharply observed studies of nature and light to a more diffused, lyrical, loosely brushed mode. He spent his later years mostly at the family's country estate in Ville-d'Avray.

54
View of Rome: The Bridge and Castel Sant'Angelo with the Cupola of Saint Peter's. 1826–27

This painting is among the best known of the many small, *plein-air* oil studies of landscape and architecture that Corot made during his first sojourn in Italy from 1825 to 1828. The artist's brief training with Michallon and Bertin in France had introduced him to the techniques of outdoor sketching as practised and advocated in theoretical writings by Pierre-Henri de Valenciennes. In Italy, Corot developed and refined these techniques, achieving an immediacy of impression and a truth to light and nature that helped revolutionize nineteenth-century landscape painting.

The view Corot selected for this picture, looking west along the Tiber toward the Ponte and Castel Sant'Angelo with Saint Peter's in the background, was a popular one treated by numerous artists working in Rome throughout the seventeenth and eighteenth centuries. It includes some of the city's most famous landmarks, and hence held much appeal for a Grand Tour clientele. Corot's composition, however, is unique. Human presence and picturesque details are almost completely eliminated in favour of a highly simplified and architectural rendering, the monumentality of which belies the painting's small size. The massive forms of the castle on the right and the houses at the left balance the long horizontal bridge with its graceful arches, accented at the very centre by Saint Peter's mighty dome. Another equal division is made between sky above and water and land below. Across this carefully structured scene falls a soft raking light that emphasizes three-dimensionality, unifies the picture's subtle range of blond tonalities, and helps create a mood of quiet repose. Thick, creamy strokes of paint build up the forms with a remarkable blend of solidity and fresh, lively handling. Essentially a sketch, the painting stands nevertheless as a complete work of art.

In later years, Corot elaborated this sketch into larger scale studio paintings of the same scene. A work measuring 40 by 53 cm, and dated by Robaut to 1828–35, is now in a private collection in New York (Robaut, no. 71bis), and another measuring 33 by 45 cm, and dated by Robaut to 1835–40, is in the Sterling and Francine Clark Art Institute, Williamstown, Massachusetts (Robaut, no. 71). Both are not only larger than the San Francisco painting but are more carefully finished, and expanded with more figures and boats. Another small sketch from Corot's first Italian period, now in the Louvre (Robaut, no. 73), depicts the view along the Tiber toward the bridge and the Castel Sant'Angelo from the opposite direction. A pencil drawing for the San Francisco picture is housed in the Boymans–van Beuningen Museum in Rotterdam. Robaut (under no. 70) records a number of copies of the painting.

SAN

oil on paper mounted on canvas
22.0 x 38.0 cm
Stamped at lower left: *Vente Corot*
Museum purchase, Archer M. Huntington Fund
1935.2

Provenance:
Corot (posthumous sale, Paris, Hôtel Drouot,
26–28 May 1875, no. 24); to M. Détrimont for M.
Tillot; Charles Tillot, Paris (his sale, Paris, Hôtel
Drouot, 14 May 1887, no. 8, withdrawn); Dr Dieulafoy,
Paris; Wildenstein & Co , New York; purchased by the
CPLH, 1935.

Literature:
Alfred Robaut, *L'oeuvre de Corot*, Paris, 1905, vol. 2,
no. 70, repr.; vol. 4, p. 195, no. 24; Jean Leymarie,
Corot: Biographical and Critical Study, Geneva, 1966,
p. 12; Colnaghi, New York, *Claude to Corot: The
Development of Landscape Painting in France*, exh.
cat., 1990, p. 284, repr.; Peter Galassi, *Corot in Italy*,
New Haven and London, 1991, pp. 156–7, repr.

Exhibited:
Paris, Universal Exposition, *L'Exposition centennale de
l'art français*, 1889, no. 156;
Philadelphia Museum of Art, *Corot, 1796–1875*, 1946,
no. 2, repr.; The Art Institute of Chicago, *Corot*, 1960,
no. 13, repr.;
The Minneapolis Institute of Arts, *The Past
Rediscovered: French Painting, 1800–1900*, 1969,
no. 15, repr.;
San Diego, Timken Art Gallery, *J.-B.-C. Corot: View of
Volterra*, 1988, no. 7, fig. 6.

Jean-Léon Gérôme
1824–1904

Jean-Léon Gérôme was born in the province of Haute-Saône, the son of a prosperous silversmith. After attending local schools, Gérôme moved to Paris in 1839 to enter the studio of Paul Delaroche. Following a year in Rome with Delaroche he studied with Charles Gleyre in 1845 and adopted his teacher's neoclassical manner for the treatment of scenes from ancient life. Gérôme's *Cock Fight* (Paris, Musée du Louvre) won a third-class medal at the Salon of 1847 and considerable critical and public attention. In 1854 the artist made the first of many trips to the Near East, and soon his treatments of oriental subjects vied in number with his classical scenes. He was awarded the Legion of Honour in 1855, appointed a professor at the Ecole des Beaux-Arts in 1863, and elected a member of the Institute of France in 1865. From this influential position as famous teacher and leading proponent of classical artistic values, Gérôme was a powerful opponent of Impressionism and the avant-garde. In 1878 he exhibited his first monumental sculpture. He remained active as a painter, sculptor and teacher until his death.

55
The Bath.   c.1880–85

The exotic, luxuriant bathing scene was a staple of orientalist iconography as inherited by Gérôme from such artists as Eugène Delacroix, Théodore Chassériau and Jean-Auguste-Dominique Ingres. It afforded an opportunity for both a voyeuristic glimpse into private precincts and the display of beautiful nudes, as well as enjoyment of the sensuous environments of Near Eastern architecture and decoration. Gérôme visited Turkey, Egypt and Greece many times to gather material and observations for his work, although his paintings freely mix invention with ethnographic accuracy. Typical of his technique is the combination in this work of tight draughtsmanship and vivid colour, as well as the stagelike realism that attempts to give authority to romantic conception. The contrasting of the two figures, one black and one white, is also a device inherited from earlier *orientalistes*. In this juxtaposition of fair and dark, occidental and oriental, privileged and underprivileged, lies an emblematic message that gives the painting considerably more force than is the case with many of Gérôme's bathing scenes.

The details of the setting provide no conclusive identification of the site, as they are typical of objects and forms found in both Turkey and Egypt. A large stone fountain carved with Islamic designs dominates the corner of the room and contrasts in its stony grey texture with the decorative richness of the tiles, textiles and other objects around it. The towels are Turkish, but the high inlaid clogs are of a type found in different eastern countries. Although the inscription high on the wall is in legible Persian and represents a chronogram such as those commonly found on Ottoman buildings, it is too fragmentary to provide much information.

Of Gérôme's numerous bathing scenes, this one is thought to be a relatively late example. It is not recorded in any of the many known photographs and photogravures of his paintings made during his lifetime. A drawing (location unknown) exists for the softly modelled nude. Given the more convincing anatomy of the slave, it is possible that she was painted from a live model. Ackerman (p. 296) sees the problems with the perspective in the background as possible evidence of an assistant's hand.

SAN

oil on canvas
73.6 x 59.6 cm
Signed at lower left: *J. L. Gerome*
Mildred Anna Williams Collection
1961.29

Provenance:
Mrs Frederick Wells; to The Minneapolis Institute of Arts, 1916; to Victor Spark, New York, 1955; purchased by the CPLH, 1961.

Literature:
Handbook of the Minneapolis Institute of Arts,

Minneapolis, 1917, p. 93, repr.; Gerald M. Ackerman, *The Life and Work of Jean-Léon Gérôme*, Paris, 1986, no. 520, colour repr. p. 117.

Exhibited:
Dayton Art Institute; The Minneapolis Institute of Arts; Baltimore, Walters Art Gallery, *Jean-Léon Gérôme*, 1972–73, no. 30, repr.; Stockton, California, The Haggin Museum, *Impressions of the Far East: Orientalist Art of the Nineteenth Century*, 1987–88, p. 30, repr.

$\mathcal{W}$illiam-Adolphe Bouguereau
1825–1905

Born in La Rochelle, William-Adolphe Bouguereau attended high school in Pons and in 1842 entered the Municipal School of Drawing and Painting at Bordeaux. In 1846 he moved to Paris and was accepted into the Ecole des Beaux-Arts. Studies in Rome from 1850 to 1854 further reinforced the classical direction of his early training. Favourable critical attention to his works at the Salons of 1854 and 1855 and at the Universal Exposition of 1855 brought a number of commissions and helped launch his career as one of the most famous and influential nineteenth-century academic painters. Bouguereau was appointed professor at the Ecole des Beaux-Arts in 1875 and elected a member of the Institute of France and an Officer of the Legion of Honour in 1876. Many other honours and commissions followed. In 1896, in his second marriage, he wed Elizabeth Jane Gardner, an American painter and longtime friend and pupil. He died in 1905 at his home in La Rochelle.

56
The Broken Pitcher. 1891

The Broken Pitcher typifies an important strain in Bouguereau's oeuvre. Following the fashion for peasant imagery established by Gustave Courbet and Jean-François Millet, among others, Bouguereau produced from the 1860s onward a long series of one- or two-figure compositions featuring attractive French and Italian country girls, often with a tinge of understated eroticism. In place of the earthier, more honest essays on harsh peasant life by Courbet and Millet emerged an idealized vision of rural tranquillity and beauty. In the case of *The Broken Pitcher*, however, the sexual innuendoes are particularly blatant. Bouguereau followed a well-established tradition, best known from Jean-Baptiste Greuze's *Broken Pitcher* of c.1775, in the use of the cracked vessel as a symbol for the loss of virginity. None too subtly, the spout of the well at the upper left provides a counterbalancing male symbol. The girl's plaintive expression leaves little doubt about the true meaning, calculated to appeal to the prurient interests of a male-dominated upper-middle-class French art market. Nevertheless, Bouguereau's sentimentality and flawless technique give the painting broad public appeal as well.

This work is recorded as having entered the collection of Mr and Mrs M. H. de Young in San Francisco by the early date of May 1893. Very likely it was the first painting by Bouguereau to reach California. Mr de Young bequeathed it to the museum bearing his name in 1926, together with a number of other paintings from his personal collection.

SAN

oil on canvas
133.0 x 85.5 cm
Signed and dated at lower left: *W-BOVGVEREAV– 1891*
Gift of M. H. de Young
53162

Provenance:
Mr and Mrs M. H. de Young, San Francisco, by May 1893; gift to the de Young, 1926.

Literature:
'Famous Paintings Owned on the West Coast',

Overland Monthly, 2nd series, 21, no. 125 (May 1893), p. 504; Marius Vachon, *W. Bouguereau*, Paris, 1900, p. 157; Richard R. Brettell and Caroline B. Brettell, *Painters and Peasants in the Nineteenth Century*, Geneva, 1983, p. 109, repr. p. 108.

Exhibited:
The New York Cultural Center; San Francisco, CPLH, *William-Adolphe Bouguereau*, 1974–75, no. 22, repr.

W·BOVGVEREAV·1891·

Camille Pissarro
1830–1903

Born in St Thomas in the Virgin Islands, Camille Pissarro was sent to boarding-school in Paris for five years. After eight years back in St Thomas and then in Caracas, he returned to Paris in 1855 to study art, working first with Anton Melbye and then at the Académie Suisse, where he met Claude Monet, Jean-Baptiste Armand Guillaumin and Paul Cézanne. Painting out of doors, he developed a personal style much influenced by Gustave Courbet and Camille Corot but with a distinct feeling for structure and contrasting tonal values in the landscape. He had his first painting accepted at the Salon of 1859, then joined Cézanne, Edouard Manet and others in the Salon des Refusés of 1863. Pissarro fled to England during the Franco-Prussian War. Back in Paris, he was a guiding force behind the first Impressionist exhibition in 1874 and participated in all seven subsequent group shows. His work gave way in the mid-1880s to a divisionist manner inspired by Georges Seurat, but he returned to a looser, less 'scientific' style in the early 1890s, and his late serial paintings of cityscapes and harbours are among his greatest achievements.

57
Harbor at Dieppe.   1902

Indicative of the attention the Impressionists paid to precise climatological and diurnal conditions in the landscapes they painted, this work was originally entitled, more descriptively, *L'Avant-port de Dieppe, à marée haute, le matin, temps gris*. The site is the outer basin of the port of Dieppe, the first of several interconnected basins reached by channels from the sea. The view is from the west looking across the *avant-port* toward bluffs in the distance surmounted by the church of Notre-Dame de Bon Secours. Over the course of several months during the summer of 1902, Pissarro painted numerous scenes around the waterways of Dieppe, attracted by the colourful activity on the docks and quays, the movement of ships, and the structured compositions of land, water and sky that these motifs offered as a backdrop for atmospheric observations.

Pissarro is documented in Dieppe through a series of letters to his son Lucien. On 11 August 1902 he wrote: 'Well, here I am in Dieppe at the Hôtel du Commerce. I have rented a room on the second floor under the arcades of the fishmarket. This is my studio'. And on 15 August: 'I am working hard and for good reason, deals are tough. . . . My motifs are very beautiful: the fishmarket, the inner harbor, the Duquesne basin, in the rain, in the sun, in the smoke, etc., etc.' By 20 October he had moved from Dieppe to Eragny, 'with my trunks full of canvases to be retouched and which I have to bring to Paris' (John Rewald, *Camille Pissarro: Letters to His Son Lucien*, Mamaroneck, NY, 1972, pp. 349–50). The Hôtel du Commerce was located in the place Nationale, one block away from the *avant-port*.

As was customary in Pissarro's later landscapes and cityscapes, the vantage-point in this picture is high. The scene must have been painted from an upper floor in a building along the quay. More or less the same perspective from the same location is seen in several other paintings from this period, documenting a changing panoply of activity and different effects of light and climate (Pissarro and Venturi, nos 1241, 1243–6). In similar groups of serial images, in his late years Pissarro surveyed the seaports at Rouen and Le Havre.

SAN

oil on canvas
46.5 x 55.3 cm
Signed and dated at lower right: *C. Pissarro, 1902*
Mildred Anna Williams Collection
1940.52

Provenance:
Gustave Cahen (his sale, Paris, Galerie Georges Petit, 24 May 1929, no. 71); to Mr and Mrs H. K. S. Williams, Paris, San Francisco, New York; gift to the CPLH, 1940.

Literature:
Ludovic R. Pissarro and Lionello Venturi, *Camille Pissarro: Son art et son oeuvre*, Paris, 1939, vol. 1, no. 1242; vol. 2, pl. 243; *Illustrated Handbook of the Collections*, CPLH, San Francisco, 1946, p. 60, repr.

Exhibited:
Paris, Galerie Durand-Ruel, *L'Oeuvre de Camille Pissarro*, 1904, no. 127;
Memphis, Tennessee, The Dixon Gallery and Gardens, *Homage to Camille Pissarro: The Last Years, 1890–1903*, 1980, no. 22, repr.

Edouard Manet
1832–1883

Born into a prosperous middle-class family, Edouard Manet spent a year in the navy before entering the studio of Thomas Couture in 1850; he stayed with this teacher until 1856. Couture encouraged strong modelling through light and dark contrasts, and copies Manet made at the Louvre, after Velázquez, Titian and Rubens among others, nurtured a painterly style of rich colour and bold brushwork. Like the realist painters, Manet chose his subjects largely from modern life. His *Déjeuner sur l'herbe*, 1863, and *Olympia*, 1863, exhibited at the Salon of 1865 (both Paris, Musée d'Orsay), created scandals, both for their unconventional subject matter and for their broad handling. A series of paintings on Spanish themes culminated with a trip to Spain in 1865 and first-hand study of works by Velázquez and Goya. At the 1867 Universal Exposition, Manet held a private exhibition, which helped solidify his leadership within the avant-garde. Charles Baudelaire, Théodore Duret and Emile Zola supported him critically. During the 1870s he worked outdoors like the Impressionists, and his work became lighter and more colourful, but he maintained hope for acceptance at the official Salons and never contributed to the Impressionist exhibitions. Success came in later years with numerous commissions and portraits. By about 1879, however, he began to feel the effects of a debilitating disease that would eventually cause his death.

58
At the Milliner's. 1881

Manet's lifelong interest in the theme of feminine sensuosity reached a height in his later years when his portraits of Isabelle Lemonnier, Méry Laurent and other friends and models captured with particular vitality an image of youthful elegance, spirit and beauty. *At the Milliner's* dates from only two or three years before the artist's death: although its exact date is not documented and in the literature has spanned the years 1879 to 1883, it is now generally ascribed to 1881. It depicts a subject from the fashionable life of modern Paris that was treated by several contemporary French artists including Pierre-Auguste Renoir, Eva Gonzalez, Henri de Toulouse-Lautrec and, on numerous occasions, Edgar Degas, that is, women in shops and boudoirs trying on hats. The title *La Modiste* given this painting in the inventory of Manet's studio, however, is misleading. Rather than a scene in a store, it seems to show a woman in the privacy of her home. It is hard to imagine a shopper wearing so revealing an off-the-shoulder dress or a wallpaper as luxurious as this in a commercial setting. Efforts to identify the sitter with one of the milliners or fashion consultants whom Manet is known to have met have therefore proved unsuccessful.

The painting may have been considered unfinished by Manet, and it remained in his studio until his posthumous sale of 1884. The almost indistinct signature at the lower left was added after his death. Some authorities have conjectured that the painting was also enhanced and retouched slightly, although evidence of another hand is difficult to detect. Indeed, despite the extreme sketchiness of certain areas of the dress and background, the picture stands as a complete artistic statement and a testament to Manet's painterly powers even in his illness-ridden later years.

Sources as diverse as Pisanello and Japanese prints have been invoked as influences for Manet's clear silhouetting of the figure's torso against the flattened decorative background. The subtle brightening of the wall just behind the woman, as though struck by sunlight through a window, helps emphasize her beautifully drawn profile and the sensuous handling of her skin. Manet's strong note of personal intimacy contrasts with Degas's treatment of the same theme, where the figures tend to recede in relation to the decorative finery and patterning of hats and ribbons.

SAN

oil on canvas
85.0 x 74.0 cm
Signed at lower left (not authentic): *E. Manet*
Mildred Anna Williams Collection
1957.3

Provenance:
Manet (posthumous sale, Paris, Hôtel Drouot, 4–5
February 1884, no. 51); to Paul Vayson, Paris; Auguste
Pellerin, Paris, by 1902; to Oscar Schmitz, Dresden, by
1914; Wildenstein & Co., New York, 1936–37; to
Mr and Mrs Edwin C. Vogel, New York, c.1937;
purchased by the CPLH, 1957.

Literature:
Théodore Duret, *Histoire d'Edouard Manet et de son*
oeuvre, Paris, 1902, no. 273; Paul Jamot and Georges
Wildenstein, *Manet*, Paris, 1932, vol. 1, no. 322; vol. 2,
fig. 132; Adolphe Tabarant, *Manet et ses oeuvres*, Paris,
1947, no. 394; Denis Rouart and Daniel Wildenstein,
Edouard Manet: Catalogue raisonné, Lausanne, 1975,
vol. 1, no. 373, repr.

Exhibited:
Paris, Galerie Bernheim-Jeune, *Manet: Trente-cinq*
tableaux de la collection Pellerin, 1910, no. 18;
Philadelphia Museum of Art; The Art Institute of
Chicago, *Edouard Manet, 1832–1883*, 1966–67, no.
165, repr.;
Paris, Grand Palais; New York, The Metropolitan
Museum of Art, *Manet, 1832–1883*, 1983, no. 213,
colour repr.

Edgar Degas
1834–1917

Hilaire Germain Edgar De Gas was born in Paris, where his father was a prominent banker. He studied at the Lycée Louis-le-Grand and briefly at law school but was most interested in becoming an artist; in 1853 he began to copy at the Louvre. He entered the Ecole des Beaux-Arts in 1855 and from 1856 to 1859 lived in Italy, studying the old masters and working from the model. In Italy again in 1860, he completed his first great painting, *The Bellelli Family* (Paris, Musée d'Orsay). His early work was mainly portraiture and large classical compositions, and he contributed regularly to the Salons from 1865 to 1870. His first sculptures date from the mid-1860s. A trip to New Orleans in 1872–73 resulted in his famous painting of the cotton buyers' office (Pau, Musée des Beaux-Arts). Back in Paris in 1874, he helped organize the first Impressionist exhibition and contributed to all but one of the subsequent seven group shows, although his many paintings of the ballet and opera, café scenes, horseraces and other aspects of metropolitan life are distinct in style and subject matter from the work of his Impressionist colleagues. About 1892 Degas began to work primarily in pastels. He was plagued by ill health and near-blindness after about 1900, and his style became increasingly broad; by 1910 he had ceased working.

59
Musicians of the Orchestra
(Portrait of Désiré Dihau). *c*.1870

This oil sketch is a study for *The Orchestra of the Paris Opéra* in the Musée d'Orsay, Paris, a work famous as one of the earliest of Degas's radically modern interpretations of theatrical subjects. The sketch differs from the final version, however, in several important aspects. The horizontal format and frontal composition of the preliminary study contrast with the verticality and diagonal viewpoint of the later work; the study is far more sketchy and monochromatic in treatment; and it lacks the strong compositional device of the railing that cuts across the bottom of the final painting and separates the viewer's space from that of the orchestra. And whereas Degas populated the orchestra in the final version with portraits of both professional musicians and various other friends and acquaintances, the sketch concentrates on one individual, the well-known bassoonist Désiré Dihau, who played at the Paris Opéra from 1862 to 1889. The other figures, with the exception of the bulky double-bass player seen from behind at the right, disappear into the flurry of Degas's loose and abstract brushwork, which gives only vague hints of torsos and instruments. To accent the rich but colouristically limited play of greys, blacks and browns, Degas has added a few light strokes of pink on the stage, suggesting faintly the legs of dancers, and a spot of bright red on the mouthpiece of the bassoon.

According to Marcel Guérin (*Degas* 1988, English and French eds, p. 162), Degas had originally intended to make a portrait of Dihau alone. No drawings or oil sketches that support this supposition are known, although the prominence of Dihau in the San Francisco study does indicate that, even if other musicians were to be added in greater detail, he was the true subject of the painting. Several pencil sketches, and modifications evident in X-rays of the final painting, document a number of different steps and changes between the oil study and the ultimate composition.

The chronological placement of the final painting, and hence of the oil sketch, has presented problems. Based on indications that the former was exhibited in 1870 in Lille during the Franco-Prussian War and again in Paris in 1871 during the Commune, both are now tentatively dated about 1870. From approximately the same time comes the similarly conceived *Orchestra Musicians*, in the Städtische Galerie im Städelschen Kunstinstitut, Frankfurt (*c*.1870–71, reworked *c*.1874–76). Together these two works constitute Degas's first ballet paintings in a format that he would later often repeat, with the viewer situated in the audience or the orchestra pit and the action on stage a distant, fragmentary backdrop. This bold perspective and cropping of the field of vision represented for Degas a major breakthrough in his efforts to introduce new immediacy to the painting of modern life. Although the available evidence is contradictory, *Musicians of the Orchestra* may have been the painting belonging to Ambroise Vollard entitled *Le Joueur de hautbois* (*The Oboe Player*) that figured in an exhibition of the Vollard collection at Knoedler Galleries in New York in 1933.

SAN

oil on canvas
50.0 x 61.0 cm
Signed at lower right: *Degas*
Mildred Anna Williams Collection
1952.69

Provenance:
Degas (posthumous sale, Paris, Galerie Georges Petit,
6–8 May 1918, no. 9); perhaps Ambroise Vollard,
Paris, by 1933; Galerie Mouradian-Vallotton, Paris, by
1938; André Weil, Paris; purchased by the CPLH, 1952.

Literature:
Paul André Lemoisne, *Degas et son oeuvre*, Paris, 1946,

vol. 2, no. 187, repr.; *Degas*, exh. cat., Paris, New York,
1988, p. 161, fig. 88 (Fr. ed.); p. 162, fig. 88 (Eng. ed.);
Jacques Lassaigne and Fiorella Minervino, *Tout l'oeuvre
peint de Degas*, Paris, 1988, no. 287, repr.

Exhibited:
Perhaps New York, M. Knoedler & Co., *Paintings from
the Ambroise Vollard Collection*, 1933, no. 17 (as *Le
Joueur de hautbois* (*The Oboe Player*));
Paris, Galerie Mouradian-Vallotton, *Degas*, 1938, no.
11;
Los Angeles County Museum, *An Exhibition of Works
by Edgar Hilaire Germain Degas*, 1958, no. 15, repr.

Henri Fantin-Latour
1836–1904

Son of the painter Théodore Fantin-Latour, Henri Fantin-Latour settled in Paris in 1841 and was trained by his father and Horace Lecoq de Boisbaudran. Key influences in his development were the example of Gustave Courbet and his study of old masters at the Louvre, where he copied almost daily until 1870. He first exhibited at the Salon of 1861 and participated in the Salon des Refusés of 1863. Fantin joined Edouard Manet, Pierre-Auguste Renoir, Frédéric Bazille and others in the avant-garde intellectual circles of Paris and commemorated leading artists, writers and musicians of the day in several group portraits, but from about 1879 he worked largely in isolation. His delicate, lyrical still lifes in the tradition of Jean-Baptiste-Siméon Chardin gave way in later years to highly romanticized compositions inspired by his love of Wagner and the opera. A personal friend of James McNeill Whistler, Fantin visited England several times and exhibited at the Royal Academy from 1862 to 1900.

60
White Rockets and Fruit. 1869

The flowers pictured in this still life are *Hesperis matronalis*, commonly known as white sweet rockets in English and *juliennes* in French. Their combination here with grapes, ripe peaches and apricots suggests that the picture was painted in late summer.

Mme Fantin-Latour, in her catalogue raisonné of her husband's work, dated the picture to 1870, whereas its inscription clearly reads '69'. It was one of Fantin's most ambitious compositions of that year. From correspondence with his agent in London, Edwin Edwards, it is known that Fantin sent the picture to Edwards in 1871 to be sold, with guarded expectations: 'I think it is good, and rather difficult to understand if one is not a painter' (Paris, etc., pp. 135–6). He set the price at 80 francs, which was low at the time for his major paintings. Edwards placed the work in the 1872 exhibition of the Society of French Artists, and although it was not listed in the catalogue it was recorded as selling for 25 guineas, or approximately 625 francs, thereby turning for Edwards, who had bought it from Fantin, a rapid and handsome profit.

Perhaps Fantin felt that the relatively severe composition of the painting, with the bouquet placed along the central vertical axis and the basket and compote of fruit arranged horizontally and symmetrically to either side, made it a more challenging picture than the syncopated arrangements of his other still lifes. It does have a classical poise that stands out even in an oeuvre noted for its serenity and balance. A similar approach is seen in certain later works including, for example, the *Climbing Roses and Peaches* of 1873 (Zurich, Stiftung Sammlung E. G. Bührle). X-rays reveal that the San Francisco picture was painted over an earlier composition by Fantin of a woman seated before an easel and a man standing behind her.

SAN

oil on canvas
56.0 x 53.3 cm
Signed and dated at upper right: *Fantin .69.*
Mildred Anna Williams Collection
1963.6

Provenance:
Edwin Edwards, London, 1871–72; Hippolyte Adam, Paris; Laurent Yeatman, Paris, by 1936; M. Knoedler & Co., New York; purchased by the CPLH, 1963.

Literature:
Victoria Fantin-Latour, *Catalogue de l'oeuvre complet (1849–1904) de Fantin-Latour*, Paris, 1911, no. 458;

Edward Lucie-Smith, *Henri Fantin-Latour*, New York, 1977, p. 161.

Exhibited:
London, Society of French Artists, third exhibition, 1872, not in cat.;
Musée de Grenoble, *Centenaire de Henri Fantin-Latour*, 1936, no. 124;
Paris, Orangerie des Tuileries, *Le Cabinet de l'amateur*, 1956, no. 50;
Paris, Grand Palais; Ottawa, The National Gallery of Canada; San Francisco, CPLH, *Fantin-Latour*, 1982–83, no. 39, colour repr. p. 39.

Paul Cézanne
1839–1906

Born in Aix-en-Provence on 19 January 1839, Paul Cézanne was groomed from an early age to assume his father's position at the family bank. Rejecting both a career in finance and the legal studies he pursued at university, however, he left the south of France in 1861 to join his longtime friend Emile Zola in Paris and to launch his artistic training. He failed the entrance examination for the Ecole des Beaux-Arts, but he frequented classes at the Académie Suisse and came to know artists in the Impressionist circle such as Camille Pissarro and Claude Monet. Cézanne's early paintings, worked in a dark and foreboding style and dominated by sexually charged images of death and violence, encountered a hostile critical reaction. He contributed in 1863 to the Salon des Refusés and, in 1874, to the first Impressionist exhibition, where he sold *House of the Hanged Man* (Paris, Musée d'Orsay). Under the guidance of Pissarro, Cézanne's early work gave way to an impressionist phase, but he quickly developed his signature style based on a blend of intense observation and architectonic compositional relationships that proved highly influential for twentieth-century formalist art. Cézanne divided his time between Paris and Provence but settled permanently in Aix in 1899. A large exhibition organized by Ambroise Vollard in 1895 and a posthumous retrospective in 1907 brought belated recognition.

61
Forest Interior. c.1898–99

Forest interiors are a common motif in Cézanne's late landscapes, providing subjects that, while often of little topographic or picturesque value, nevertheless are dramatized by his constructive transformations of nature. The painting in The Fine Arts Museums, dating most likely from about 1898 to 1899, exhibits many of the most characteristic elements of these late works: patterned brushstrokes that build into compositional units; a thin application of paint for greater luminosity; a simplification of solid forms into geometric shapes; colouristic richness; and an overall emphasis on balanced structure. The composition is built around a complex set of movements and contrasts, with rocks thrusting upward against the verticals of the trees and with strong diagonals crossing at the centre, where a curving tree trunk marks a focal point toward which the spaces on either side collapse. Green and ochre are the primary colour chords, subtly woven together with many small strokes that harmonize both tone and texture.

Although the preponderance of Cézanne's late landscapes depict sites around his native Aix, occasionally before 1900 he continued to work in the north, and the locale of *Forest Interior* has remained a subject of debate. Lionello Venturi (1936) catalogued this work as *Rochers dans le parc du Château Noir*, and most later writers have followed his lead in ascribing it to the forested slopes surrounding the so-called Château Noir, where Cézanne so often worked. John Rewald, however, remains convinced that the site is the Forest of Fontainebleau. He has written that

> the rock-strewn slope could also be the one that ascends toward the ridge behind Château Noir, except that there the rocks and trees are generally not quite as dense nor the tree trunks as red. . . . Some of the boulders show ocher tints not unlike the tones of those near the Bibémus quarry; but the foliage of the trees is of a sharp green, in contrast to the dark fir trees around Château Noir, and the pale blue sky is quite unlike that of Provence (*Cézanne: The Late Work*, no. 22).

In subsequent correspondence (1990), Rewald reiterated his opinion that the locale is Fontainebleau, where Cézanne is known to have worked during a long northern sojourn from the summer of 1898 to the autumn of 1899.

Several paintings from the same period either conclusively or tentatively identified as northern sites provide a basis for comparison. These include *Bend in the Road at Montgeroult* (private collection; Venturi, no. 668), *Lake Annecy* (London, Courtauld Institute Galleries; Venturi, no. 762), *Rocks in the Forest* (New York, The Metropolitan Museum of Art; Venturi, no. 673, argued by Rewald to derive from Fontainebleau), and another *Rocks in the Forest* (Zurich, Kunsthaus; Venturi, no. 674). In general, however, these works exhibit a more pervasively blue-green palette and a softer sense of light than this painting, whose strongly ochre foreground, reddish trees and light green foliage seem to place it closer to such well-known canvases as *Cistern in the Park at Château Noir* (Henry Pearlman estate; Venturi, no. 780) and *Forest of Château Noir* (Philadelphia Museum of Art; Venturi, no. 768).   SAN

oil on canvas
60.0 x 81.0 cm
Mildred Anna Williams Collection
1977.4

Provenance:
Ambroise Vollard, Paris; Louis Bernard, Paris, sold 29
September 1916; to Galerie Bernheim-Jeune, Paris, 29
September 1916 – 31 December 1917; to Galerie
Bernheim-Jeune, Lausanne; Siegmund Gildemeister,
Bremen and Hamburg, by 1927; Alfred Gold, Paris, by
1930; Mrs Harris Jonas, New York, by 1947; to William
Beadleston, Inc., New York; purchased by TFAMSF,
1977.

Literature:
Julius Meier-Graefe, *Cézanne*, New York, 1927, pl. 35;
Lionello Venturi, *Cézanne: Son art, son oeuvre*, Paris,
1936, vol. 1. no. 784; vol. 2, pl. 258; Ian Dunlop and
Sandra Orienti, *The Complete Paintings of Cézanne*,
New York, 1970, no. 712, repr.; John Rewald, *Cézanne:
A Biography*, New York, 1986, p. 247, colour repr.

Exhibited:
Paris, Galerie Bernheim-Jeune, *Paul Cézanne*, 1924;
New York, Wildenstein & Co., *Cézanne*, 1947, no. 64;
New York, The Museum of Modern Art; Houston, The
Museum of Fine Arts; Paris, Grand Palais, *Cézanne:
The Late Work*, 1977 – 78, no. 22, pl. 51;
Aix-en-Provence, Musée Granet, *Sainte-Victoire:
Cézanne*, 1990, no. 32, colour repr.

Alfred Sisley
1839–1899

Alfred Sisley was born in Dunkirk to parents of Anglo-French descent. His father worked in the silk business and as an exporter of artificial flowers. From 1857 to 1861, Sisley lived in London and trained for a career in business. A growing interest in art, however, led him to return to Paris in 1862 and to enter the studio of Charles Gleyre, where he met Claude Monet, Pierre-Auguste Renoir and Frédéric Bazille with whom he painted in the Forest of Fontainebleau under the influence of Camille Corot and Charles-Francois Daubigny. Together they formed the vanguard of the Impressionist movement. Sisley exhibited at the Salons of 1866, 1868 and 1870, and at the Impressionist exhibitions of 1874, 1876, 1877 and 1882. The Franco-Prussian War brought financial ruin to Sisley's father and left the artist with no means of support, although in about 1872 Durand-Ruel began to handle his work. One-person exhibitions were organized by Durand-Ruel in Paris in 1883 and New York in 1889, but sales remained scarce. During the 1870s and early 1880s, Sisley lived and worked in various locations in Paris, the Seine valley and England as well. In 1882 he moved to Moret-sur-Loing, then to Sablons in 1883, and finally back to Moret-sur-Loing in 1889. Plagued by ill health in his later years, he died in 1899 after a long battle with cancer.

62
Acacia Tree in Blossom. 1895

By 1895 Sisley's health was failing and his output became more limited. His catalogue raisonné lists only six paintings for this year, of which four are scenes of wooded fields with haystacks. These presumably were all done at locations near Sisley's home in Moret-sur-Loing, not far from Fontainebleau. After 1889 he rarely travelled from this region.

In *Acacia Tree in Blossom,* a convincing impression is created of a hot late-summer day, with a bright sky and the sun high overhead. Reviving a compositional device he had used often in the past, Sisley leads the eye diagonally into the landscape along a steeply receding path. In contrast, spatial recession on the right is blocked by the large and dominant flowering tree and the haystack behind it, which stress the foreground plane of the painting and nearly fill the view with bright, dappled colour. For anecdotal effect, Sisley has added the farm woman standing with her rake on the path and another figure with a horse-drawn wagon at the right.

Sisley's later work in general is characterized by smaller, choppier brushstrokes and brighter colour. Here, the slightly astringent yellows of the acacia blossoms and the reddish purples of the tree trunk and hayricks predominate. Red is used throughout as an accent, even in the sky, where purple tones intermingle with blue, recalling distantly the coloration of Renoir's landscapes of the 1880s.

SAN

oil on canvas
54.5 x 65.5 cm
Signed and dated at lower right: *Sisley. 95*
Bequest of Marco F. Hellman
1974.7

Provenance:
F. Stumpf, Paris (his sale, Paris, Galerie Georges Petit, 7 May 1906, no. 75); Léon Orsodi, Paris (his sale, Paris, Hôtel Drouot, 25 May 1923, no. 68); René Keller, Paris; Justin K. Thannhauser, New York; private collection; Dalzell Hatfield Galleries, Los Angeles, until 1956; to

Mr and Mrs Marco F. Hellman, San Francisco; bequeathed to TFAMSF, 1974.

Literature:
François Daulte, *Alfred Sisley: Catalogue raisonné de l'oeuvre peint,* Paris, 1959, no. 841, repr.

Exhibited:
San Francisco Museum of Modern Art, *Modern Masters in West Coast Collections,* 1960;
Tokyo, Isetan Museum of Art; Fukuoka Museum of Art; Nara Prefectural Museum, *Alfred Sisley Retrospective,* 1985, no. 50, repr.

Claude Monet
1840–1926

Born in Paris in 1840, Claude Monet moved with his family to Le Havre in 1845. He attended public school in Le Havre and learned to draw from François-Charles Ochard, although the early instruction he received from Eugène Boudin was more critical. In 1859 Monet travelled to Paris, where he attended the Académie Suisse and began a friendship with the older Camille Pissarro. He received formal art training in 1863 in the studio of Charles Gleyre, where he met Frédéric Bazille, Pierre-Auguste Renoir and Alfred Sisley. Despite the acceptance of his paintings at the Salons of 1865 and 1866, he suffered severe financial problems. In 1873 Monet and other artists in his circle formed the Société Anonyme Coopérative d'Artistes–Peintres–Sculpteurs–Graveurs, which in 1874 held its first group show, later known as the first Impressionist exhibition. Monet exhibited *Impression: Sunrise* (Paris, Musée Marmottan), the painting from which the Impressionists derived their name. He also participated in the second (1876), third (1877), fourth (1879) and seventh (1882) group shows. During his career, he painted in a number of locations throughout France as well as in London, Venice, the Low Countries and Scandinavia. He established studios at Argenteuil (1871), then at Vétheuil (1878) and finally at Giverny (1883), where he bought a house and property in 1890 and began to concentrate on the paintings of his gardens that would later become so famous. As Monet grew older, his eyesight deteriorated, but despite his failing vision he continued to paint until his death in 1926. His last years were preoccupied by his grand cycles of water lily paintings, one of which was installed after his death in the Musée de l'Orangerie in Paris.

63
Water Lilies.   *c.*1914–17

According to the eyewitness account of Maurice Guillemot, Monet had begun working on the first of his water lily paintings by 1897 (see Wildenstein, p. 150). From then until his death, the water lily ponds and surrounding vegetation in his garden at Giverny provided an inexhaustible source of inspiration, as he concentrated more and more exclusively on this subject and on the purified experience of colour, light, reflection and atmosphere that his focused examinations offered.

Until about 1914, the sizes of the water lily paintings were generally restricted to one metre or less in either dimension. In 1915 Monet completed a third and larger studio on his property that permitted work on a grander scale. San Francisco's painting, measuring 180 by 146.5 cm, has been dated by Daniel Wildenstein to 1914–17, during the first phase of the artist's expanded formats. Its loose and energetic handling indicates an advanced stage of development, although its style is still not as abstract as Monet's style would later become. The flowers here are open and deep red in colour as they would be at the height of summer. Typically for the works of this period, Monet's paint application varies between thick impastos and thin washes. Reflections of clouds intermingle with the surface vegetation and flashes of light from deep within the pond, as Monet's horizonless composition blurs the distinctions between surface and depth, tangible and intangible, and solid and void.

Physical evidence indicates that this painting may have been cut down on one side, perhaps from a considerably larger canvas. Thinly painted margins on the top, bottom and right side contrast with the solidly painted left edge. Other instances of water lily paintings having been cut are known (see Wildenstein, no. 1893), but, in this case, no related fragment has been identified.

SAN

oil on canvas
180.0 x 146.5 cm
Mildred Anna Williams Collection
1973.3

Provenance:
Claude Monet's studio, Giverny; to Michel Monet,
Giverny; to Katia Granoff, Paris, c.1955; to John
Huston, Los Angeles and Ireland, 1956–70; to Spencer
A. Samuels & Co., New York, 1971; to Mrs Ira Haupt
(née Enid Annenberg), 1971–72; to Spencer A.
Samuels & Co., New York, 1973; purchased by
TFAMSF, 1973.

Literature:
Denis Rouart and Jean-Dominique Rey, *Monet:
Nymphéas*, Paris, 1972, n.p., repr.; Daniel Wildenstein,
Claude Monet: Biographie et catalogue raisonné, Paris,
1985, vol. 4, no. 1788, repr.

Exhibited:
San Francisco, CPLH; Santa Barbara Museum of Art;
Fine Arts Gallery of San Diego, *Claude Monet:
Paintings in California Collections*, 1974, no. 11,
colour repr.;
The Art Institute of Chicago, *Paintings by Monet*, 1975,
no. 118, repr.;
Kunstmuseum Basel, *Claude Monet: Nymphéas*, 1986,
no. 30, colour pl. 68.

$\mathcal{P}$ierre-Auguste Renoir
1841–1919

Son of a tailor and a dressmaker, Pierre-Auguste Renoir moved with his family from Limoges to Paris in 1844. From 1854 to 1858 he was apprenticed to a porcelain manufacturer, where he painted rococo-style decorations. In 1862–63 he attended the Ecole des Beaux-Arts in the studio of Charles Gleyre, where he met Alfred Sisley, Camille Pissarro, Claude Monet and Henri Fantin-Latour. Renoir first exhibited at the Salon of 1864 and began at about this time to work out of doors. Gustave Courbet, Camille Corot and Charles-François Daubigny were important early influences, although Renoir's progress toward a more vivid and sketchy style was encouraged by the work of Monet and of Edouard Manet. He participated in the first Impressionist exhibition of 1874 but subsequently in only the second, third and seventh group shows. In 1881–82 Renoir travelled to Algeria and Italy, where his exposure to ancient and Renaissance art led him to introduce into his impressionism a new linear and sculptural direction. After he had endured years of financial struggle, a retrospective at Durand-Ruel in 1892 signalled greater popular success. Although his health began to fail in the late 1890s, Renoir continued to paint, and even to experiment with sculpture, until his death.

64
Madame Clémentine Valensi Stora (L'Algérienne). 1870

Madame Clémentine Valensi Stora dates from the same year as Renoir's great *Woman of Algiers* (Washington, DC, National Gallery of Art) and partakes of the same intense interest in exotic North African themes that inspired his *Parisian Women in Algerian Dress* of 1872 (Tokyo, National Museum of Western Art) and his copy after Eugène Delacroix's *Jewish Wedding* from about 1875 (Worcester, Mass., Worcester Art Museum). Coming at a time when Renoir's work in general was moving away from the heavier forms and more sombre coloration of Courbet and Corot, this *orientaliste* tendency corresponded with the lightening of palette and loosening of brushwork that were key to Renoir's early Impressionist style. Unlike his Algerian genre paintings and costume studies, however, this picture is most definitely a portrait. The sitter is Clémentine Valensi Stora (1845/1847–1917), the Tunisian-born wife of a dealer in carpets and antiques whose shop, Au Pacha, on the boulevard des Italiens, was well known among artists for its lavish displays of oriental rugs. Renoir apparently was struck by the beauty of Mme Stora and asked her to pose for him. Dressed in a traditional Algerian costume and placed before a hanging kilim carpet, she sits impassively, enmeshed in the thick rivulets of paint with which Renoir built up the free and energetic play of materials and decoration surrounding the more carefully modelled face. Mme Stora's dark-eyed North African features must indeed have been striking, as she was also painted by Benjamin Constant and Constant-Joseph Brochard, among others.

In his *Diary of an Art Collector*, René Gimpel recorded in a passage from 1918 that the painter Paul-César Helleu had discovered this painting at the home of the Storas, who considered it awful (presumably for its modernity), and that he had purchased it for three hundred francs. The much-preferred, more traditional portraits by Constant and Brochard remained in family hands. The present work was not included in the Salon of 1870, as is sometimes reported, but surfaced publicly with its exhibition in Marseilles in 1906, although the name of the sitter had at that point been forgotten.

oil on canvas
81.5 x 59.6 cm
Signed and dated at lower right: *A. Renoir .70.*
Gift of Mr. and Mrs. Prentis Cobb Hale in honor of Thomas Carr Howe, Jr.
1966.47

Provenance:
Stora family; to Paul-César Helleu, Paris, 1894; to Claude Monet, Giverny, by 1906; to Michel Monet, Giverny, 1926; Galerie Bernheim-Jeune, Paris, by 1938; Reid and Lefevre and William Hallsborough Ltd., London, by 1952; Prentis Cobb Hale, San Francisco; gift to the CPLH, 1966.

Literature:
Ambroise Vollard, *Tableaux, pastels et dessins de*

Pierre- Auguste Renoir, Paris, 1918, no. 378, repr.; René Gimpel, *Diary of an Art Collector*, New York, 1963, p. 62; François Daulte, *Auguste Renoir: Catalogue raisonné de l'oeuvre peint*, Lausanne, 1971, vol. 1, no. 47, repr.

Exhibited:
Marseilles, Exposition nationale coloniale, *L'Exposition rétrospective des orientalistes français*, 1906, no. 52; Paris, Galerie Bernheim-Jeune, *Renoir: Portraitiste*, 1938, no. 1, repr.; London, The Tate Gallery, *Renoir*, 1953, no. 3, repr.; The Art Institute of Chicago, *Paintings by Renoir*, 1973, no. 8, repr.; London, Hayward Art Gallery; Paris, Grand Palais; Boston, Museum of Fine Arts, *Renoir*, 1985–86, no. 17, colour repr. p. 53.

65

Landscape at Beaulieu. 1893

Although inscribed *97*, this work can be redated on documentary grounds to 1893. In the spring of that year, Renoir made a visit to Beaulieu on the Mediterranean coast east of Nice and recorded in a letter of 27 April that he was working hard on a landscape, possibly this particular one; no corresponding trip is known for 1897. Renoir kept this painting until 1914, when he deposited it with the Durand-Ruel gallery, which purchased it in 1917. The gallery's early documentary photograph shows that the painting was not signed. Renoir was presumably asked to sign it in 1917 but very likely gave it an incorrect date owing to a faulty memory.

Unusually large for Renoir's landscapes of the 1890s, this work recalls the bright, somewhat acrid colours and wildly luxuriant foliage that had emerged in his tropical Algerian landscapes of 1881–82. A basic shift of theme has occurred, however. As opposed to the earlier views of uninhabited, untamed nature, the setting here seems to be a park or a private garden. The low masonry wall that cuts across the foreground not only adds compositional structure within Renoir's exuberant colour and brushwork but joins with the motif of the two casual strollers at the picture's centre to signal the cultivation of nature through a civilizing, ordering human presence.

SAN

oil on canvas
65.0 x 81.0 cm
Signed and dated (inaccurately?) at lower right: *Renoir.
97*
Mildred Anna Williams Collection
1944.9

Provenance:
Deposited by Renoir at Galerie Durand-Ruel, Paris, 1914; purchased by Durand-Ruel, 1917; purchased by the CPLH from Durand-Ruel, New York, 1944.

Literature:
Jermayne MacAgy, '*Landscape at Beaulieu* by Pierre-Auguste Renoir', *Bulletin CPLH* 2, no. 9 (December 1944), pp. 66–70.

Exhibited:
New York, Durand-Ruel Galleries, *Exhibition of Paintings by Renoir*, 1918, no. 23;
The Art Institute of Chicago, *Paintings by Renoir*, 1973, no. 68, repr.;
London, Hayward Art Gallery; Paris, Grand Palais; Boston, Museum of Fine Arts, *Renoir*, 1985–86, no. 92, colour repr. p. 135.

Louis-Maurice Boutet de Monvel
1850–1913

Born on 15 October 1850 in Orléans to a family long involved in the theatre, Louis-Maurice Boutet de Monvel was encouraged in his desires to become an artist. At age nineteen, he entered the studio of Alexandre Cabanel. After military service in the Franco-Prussian War, he resumed his academic training with Jules Lefebvre and Gustave Boulanger and in 1875 began studies with Charles-Emile Carolus-Duran. Boutet de Monvel first exhibited at the Salon of 1874. He won a second-class medal in 1880 and later a gold medal at the Paris Exposition of 1900. Although known at first for his portraits, landscapes and oriental subjects, he achieved his fame as an illustrator of children's books and historical literature. A commission from Charles Delagrave in 1880 for illustrations for his new children's magazine, *Saint Nicolas: Journal illustré pour garçons et filles*, launched Boutet de Monvel's new career. Many other projects followed, the most famous being his pictorial life of Joan of Arc, in both book form and large panels. Developing his watercolour technique, he continued to paint portraits, often in small scale in a meticulous style. A major exhibition and tour of the artist's work took place in the United States in 1899.

66
Portrait of Paul Mounet. *c.*1875

Best known as an illustrator of historical and children's literature, Boutet de Monvel was also a skilled portraitist, whose style evolved considerably during his lengthy career in reflection of different artistic fashions. The present work dates from an early stage in the artist's development, when he was still strongly influenced by both Edgar Degas and his teacher at the time, Charles-Emile Carolus-Duran. From Carolus-Duran comes the formal quality of the portrait, with its narrow, three-quarter-length format, casual but still aristocratic bearing, and evocation of historical types, most notably in the work of Velázquez; from Degas derive the warm, almost monochromatic palette and sketchy handling. Forms are confidently defined with thin, loosely brushed washes of paint that leave a good deal of underlying ground colour exposed. Although the head and hand of the sitter are built up in thicker strokes of greys and flesh tones, the modelling even here is vivacious and loose. The handling of clothing is especially sketchy, and a few broad, summary strokes are added in the background at the left to suggest drapery or some other element of setting.

The subject has been identified through the painting's inscription as the actor Paul Mounet, younger brother of the famous tragedian Jean Mounet-Sully. Boutet de Monvel exhibited at the Salon of 1875 a portrait of Mounet-Sully, very possibly the portrait pictured on the artist's easel in a photograph of his studio taken in 1876 (published in *Maurice Boutet de Monvel: Master of French Illustration and Portraiture*, Washington, DC, 1987, p. 4). Similar profile views are found in other contemporary images of Mounet-Sully. The painting in the photograph corresponds very closely to the Museums' portrait in both style and scale, as well as in the dress of the sitter, and even the pose is related. These similarities argue not only for a dating of the San Francisco portrait to this same general period but also for the likelihood that the two works depict brothers.

Paul Mounet was born in Bergerac in 1847 and died in Paris in 1922. Although trained as a doctor, he abandoned his medical career at thirty-three to become an actor. From 1880, he appeared at the Odéon Theatre in Paris in various dramatic roles, and in 1889 he entered the Comédie-Française, where he was named professor in 1898, and where he joined forces with his famous brother.

SAN

oil on canvas
113.7 x 70.0 cm
Signed and inscribed at lower left: *M B. de Monvel/a l'ami P. Mounet*
Museum purchase, Art Trust Fund and Mr. and Mrs. Vernon J. McKale Fund
1985.49

Provenance:
Ferdinand Cormon, France; by descent to Madeleine

Cauderc, France (Succession Cormon sale, Paris, Nouveau Drouot, 7–8 March 1984, no. 112); to Wheelock Whitney & Co., New York; purchased by TFAMSF, 1985.

Literature:
Emmanuel Bénézit, *Dictionnaire critique et documentaire des peintres, sculpteurs, dessinateurs et graveurs*, 3rd ed., Paris, 1976, vol. 2, p. 247.

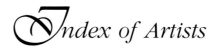

Index of Artists

Entries are listed here by catalogue number